SCHOLASTIC

Follow-the-Directions
Solve & Draw Math

Grades 6–8

Merideth Anderson

Edited by Sarah Longhi
Designed and illustrated by Kelli Thompson
Cover design by Ka-Yeon Kim-Li

ISBN-13: 978-0-545-10839-3
ISBN-10: 0-545-10839-X

Copyright © 2009 by Merideth Anderson
All rights reserved. Published by Scholastic Inc.
Printed in the U.S.A.

1 2 3 4 5 6 7 8 9 10   40   15 14 13 12 11 10 09

New York • Toronto • London • Auckland • Sydney
Mexico City • New Delhi • Hong Kong • Buenos Aires

Teaching *Resources*

Contents x + < > ＝ ¼ – % ÷ $ x + < > ＝ ¼ – %

Introduction

This book includes 15 standards-based activities that combine math skills practice with fun, follow-the-directions drawing. In addition, as students read the directions for completing the drawing, they practice critical reading and sequencing skills. Below is a short guide to what you'll find in each activity, tips for making your lesson successful, an NCTM standards chart, and a reference page for students.

Teacher Page

Each teacher page includes the following elements:

* Skill Focus: objectives of the lesson
* Materials: a list of materials needed to complete the activity
* Vocabulary: key terms used throughout the activity
* Getting Started: tips to help you assist students, specific to the lesson
* Fast Finishers: short activities for students who finish before others

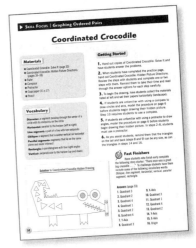

Teacher page for Coordinated Crocodile (page 32)

Solve It

The Solve It page gives students 15 or 16 math problems that target the focus math skill. Accurate answers give students the key to solving the Hidden Picture. *Make sure that students have answered these questions prior to completing the Hidden Picture Directions pages to ensure that they are working the problems out completely and not simply guessing.*

Hidden Picture Directions

The Hidden Picture Directions page consists of 15 or 16 step-by-step directions to complete the hidden picture. Students use their answers from the Solve It questions to follow the correct set of steps. Some steps are very simple while others give more detail. Encourage students to take their time and read each direction very thoroughly.

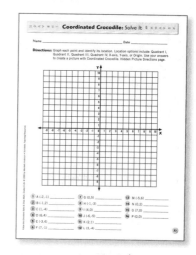

Solve It for Coordinated Crocodile (page 33)

Tips for a Successful Lesson

Here are some ways to make the activities a success:

* Before starting the activity, have students collect all the supplies they'll need to complete it.
* Make sure students know each vocabulary word listed on the teacher page prior to starting the activity.
* Have students complete the Solve It page before you hand out the Hidden Picture Directions pages. (This prevents them from guessing at the answers to complete the drawing.)
* Encourage students to double-check their answers before drawing.
* Emphasize the importance of reading the entire set of directions before drawing.
* Have students do all of their work in pencil. They can color their drawings once they've checked that they have the correct solution.

Hidden Picture Directions for Coordinated Crocodile (pages 34–36)

Step/Question	If your answer is . . .	
① Make the body.	**Quadrant 3:** • From the bottom left corner of the page, measure up 3¾ in. and then right 3 in. Make a mark. • From this point, draw a 9¼-in. horizontal line segment to the right.	**Quadrant 4:** • From the center of the page, draw an 8-in. horizontal line segment, extending left.
② Make the body.	**Quadrant 4:** • Place your pencil on the right endpoint of the segment you drew in step 1. • Draw a 2-in. vertical segment extending up.	**Quadrant 2:** • Use the segment you drew in step 1 as a base and its right endpoint as a vertex. Measure a 174° angle, drawing a 3¾-in. oblique line segment extending up and to the right.

Illustrations on the Hidden Picture Directions pages provide students with visual clues to assist them with following the written directions. When necessary, numbers are included in the drawings to show the current step in relation to previous steps. Please note that these illustrations are not drawn to scale.

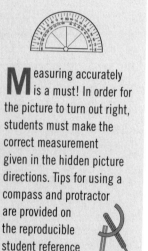

Measuring accurately is a must! In order for the picture to turn out right, students must make the correct measurement given in the hidden picture directions. Tips for using a compass and protractor are provided on the reproducible student reference sheet on page 6.

✳ Have students label each step when drawing. This will help them complete later steps. For example, an activity may direct students to draw a segment in step 1 and then, in step 10, have them locate one endpoint of the segment from step 1. Having students label the steps will also help you assist them and locate any mistakes easily.

✳ As students follow the written directions, make sure they take measurements precisely and accurately—a correct solution depends on it!

✳ To check whether their pictures have turned out as designed, have students compare their drawing with that of a classmate. You might also offer an enlarged copy of the picture answer key on the teacher page. If there is a discrepancy, locate the step (and the problem from the Solve It page) where the student has drawn part of the picture differently.

Ideas for Differentiation

Here are some ways to help students who learn and work at different paces:

For students who may need more assistance than others:

✳ Check students' Solve It pages before they read the picture directions.

✳ Read aloud the directions as students follow along.

✳ Have students highlight the steps they need to follow (or cross out the wrong choices) to help them focus on the right steps.

✳ Give students a preview of the finished drawing before they start drawing.

✳ Complete a selected number of steps with students to help them get started with their picture.

✳ Pair struggling students with higher-skill students who can assist with checking problems and reading the directions.

For students who excel at math and need an extra challenge:

✳ High-level students who strive for perfection may ask many questions while completing the drawing. Limit these questions to three or give limited help to these students, as the drawing will reveal itself in the end.

✳ Have students work in pairs or independently to create their own hidden-picture activity with a set of five skills items connected with five directions. Remind them to keep the drawing directions simple.

NCTM Standards

This chart shows how the activities in this book are aligned to standards set by the National Council of Teachers of Mathematics.

Activity	Number and Operations	Algebra	Geometry	Measurement	Data Analysis and Probability	Problem Solving	Communications	Representations	Connections
Fishy Operations	●			●	●		●	●	●
School Bus Statistics	●	●		●	●	●	●	●	●
Batty 'Bout Decimals	●			●	●		●	●	●
Fine Feathered Equations	●	●		●	●		●	●	●
Rounding Skills to Crow About	●			●	●		●	●	●
Coordinated Crocodile			●	●	●		●	●	●
Winter Numberland	●			●	●		●	●	●
Snow-Day Decimals	●			●	●		●	●	●
Dazzling Division	●			●	●		●	●	●
Icky Integers	●			●	●		●	●	●
Expressions Are Doggone Fun	●	●		●	●		●	●	●
Fancy Over Fractions	●	●		●	●		●	●	●
Luck o' the Integer	●			●	●		●	●	●
Racing Through Percents	●			●	●		●	●	●
Fraction Factions	●	●		●	●		●	●	●

Compass and Protractor Skills

You'll use a compass and a protractor for drawing circles, arcs, angles, and more in your hidden pictures. Practice these pointers to ace these tools.

Compass Pointers

＊ To draw a circle: Set the compass to the length of the circle's radius, or half of the circle's diameter. (Use a ruler to measure the distance between the pencil tip and the compass tip.) For example, to make a circle with a 6-inch diameter, set the compass to 3 inches.

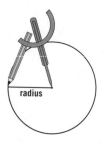 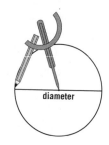

＊ To draw large circles: First set your compass to the correct radius. Then fold your paper in half. Put the compass tip on the fold where you want the midpoint of the circle to be and turn the paper (not the compass). When you've drawn half the circle, flip the paper over, put the compass on the same point along the fold and draw the other half, as shown below.

  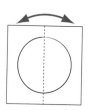

＊ To draw arcs: Place the pencil tip on the end of the segment where the arc will begin. Place the compass tip at a point horizontal to the pencil, and draw a half-circle, ending 180° from where you started, as shown below.

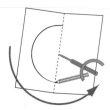

Protractor Pointers

＊ To draw angles: Line up your protractor with the base line of the angle or the endpoint given. Mark your angle according to the measurement given. Now use the straight edge of the protractor or a ruler to draw the line segment from the endpoint of the base to the mark you made. See the example below.

＊ To get the right measurement: Notice that there are two sets of numbers on a protractor. If an angle opens to the left, use the bottom set of numbers, but if the angle opens to the right, use the top set of numbers. See the example below, which shows a 50° angle opening to the left and to the right.

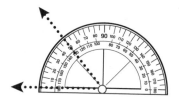

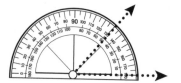 **Try It!**
On the back of this page, practice drawing circles and arcs of various sizes. Then practice drawing the following angles: 75°, 90°, 110°, 37°, 143°.

Follow-the-Directions Solve & Draw Math, Grades 6–8 • © 2009 by Merideth Anderson • Scholastic Teaching Resources

Fishy Operations

Materials

* Fishy Operations: Solve It (page 8)
* Fishy Operations: Hidden Picture Directions
  (pages 9–11)
* Ruler
* Compass
* Protractor
* Copy paper (8½ x 14 or larger)
* Pencil

Vocabulary

Trapezoid: a four-sided figure with two parallel and two nonparallel sides

Oblique lines: lines that are neither vertical nor horizontal

Arc: a part of a circle

Line segment: a part of a line with two endpoints

Vertical line: a line perpendicular to the horizon (up and down)

Getting Started

1. Hand out copies of Fishy Operations: Solve It and have students answer the problems.

2. When students have completed the practice page, hand out Fishy Operations: Hidden Picture Directions. Review the steps with students and complete one or two steps with them, reminding them to take their time and read through the steps carefully.

3. To begin the drawing, have students collect the materials listed at left and set their papers horizontally (landscape).

4. If students are unfamiliar with using a compass to draw circles and arcs, model the procedure on page 6 before they begin drawing their hidden picture. Steps 3, 4, 7, and 10 require the use of a compass.

5. As you assist students, keep in mind that triangles on the tail can be any even number and in any pattern, and stripes on the body can be any even number.

Fast Finishers

Have students who finish early write a story about a day in the life of a fish. The story should be told in the point of view of the fish just drawn. To challenge students, have them include some of these math vocabulary terms: *trapezoid, arc, triangle, vertical, horizontal, oblique lines, diameter, circle, even, odd.*

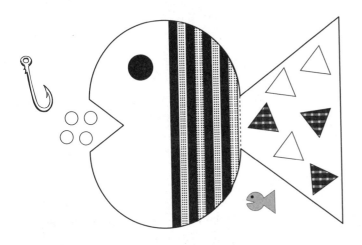

Solution to Fishy Operations Hidden Drawing

Answers (page 8)

1. 9,252	9. 6,622
2. 2,759	10. 34,400
3. 12,480	11. 35,002
4. 4,895	12. 31,164
5. 2,980	13. 60 r5
6. 6,828	14. 705 r4
7. 176	15. 47 r11
8. 2,080	16. 34 r21

Name _____ Date _____

Directions: Solve each problem and show your work.

1 8,228 + 1,024	**2** 2,308 + 451	**3** 7,121 + 5,359	**4** 786 + 4,109
5 3,789 − 809	**6** 7,411 − 583	**7** 601 − 425	**8** 4,178 − 2,098
9 946 × 7	**10** 430 × 80	**11** 946 × 37	**12** 371 × 84
13 485 ÷ 8	**14** 4,939 ÷ 7	**15** 1,609 ÷ 34	**16** 2,129 ÷ 62

Follow-the-Directions Solve & Draw Math, Grades 6–8 • © 2009 by Merideth Anderson • Scholastic Teaching Resources

Directions: Use your answers to Fishy Operations: Solve It to choose an answer for each step below. One step at a time, follow the directions to reveal the hidden picture!

Step/Question	If your answer is . . .	
1 Make the tail.	**9,252:** • Draw a fish tail shaped like a trapezoid. • The left side will measure 2 in., the right side 8⅛ in., and the other two sides 5 in. • The right side of the trapezoid should be 2 in. from the right side of the paper.	**10,252:** • Draw a fish tail shaped like a trapezoid. • The left side will measure 10⅛ in., the right side 4 in., and the other two sides 5 in. • The right side of the trapezoid should be 5 in. from the right side of the paper.
2 Finish the tail. or	**6,818:** • Trace darkly over the 2-in. line segment you drew in step 1.	**2,759:** • Erase the 2-in. line segment you drew in step 1.
3 Make the body.	**12,480:** • Set your compass for a 6-in.-diameter circle. • Place the pencil tip of the compass at the low end of the top 5-in. segment you drew in step 1. • Draw a half circle, or arc, starting with your pencil tip at the low end moving left.	**12,409:** • Set your compass for a 4-in.-diameter circle. • Place the pencil tip of the compass at the low end of the top 5-in. segment you drew in step 1. • Draw a half circle, or arc, moving right.
4 Make the belly.	**4,895:** • Set your compass for a 6-in.-diameter circle. • Place the pencil tip of the compass at the upper end of the bottom 5-in. segment you drew in step 1. • Draw a half circle, or arc, moving left.	**4,815:** • Set your compass for a 4-in.-diameter circle. • Place the pencil tip of the compass at the upper end of the bottom 5-in. segment you drew in step 1. • Draw a half circle, or arc, moving left.

Step/Question	If your answer is . . .	
5 Make the mouth.	**2,980:** • Place your pencil at the left endpoint of the top arc you drew in step 3. • Draw a 1-in. oblique line segment moving towards the bottom right-hand corner of the page.	**3,180:** • Place your pencil at the left endpoint of the top arc you drew in step 3. • Draw a 1½-in. oblique line segment moving toward the bottom right-hand corner of the page.
6 Make the mouth.	**7,172:** • Place your pencil at the end-point of the bottom arc you drew in step 4. • Draw a 1½-in. oblique line segment that connects to the bottom endpoint of the segment you drew in step 5.	**6,828:** • Place your pencil at the end-point of the bottom arc you drew in step 4. • Draw a 1-in. oblique line segment that connects to the bottom endpoint of the segment you drew in step 5.
7 Make the eye.	**176:** • Set your compass for a 1-in.-diameter circle. • Draw a circle above the oblique line segment you drew in step 5.	**276:** • Set your compass for a ½ in.-diameter circle. • Draw a circle above the oblique line segment you drew in step 5.
8 Decorate the body.	**2,080:** • Draw an even number of vertical stripes on the body (not the tail!) of the fish.	**2,120:** • Draw an odd number of horizontal stripes on the body (not the tail!) of the fish.
9 Decorate the tail.	**6,622:** • Use an even number of triangles to decorate the tail.	**6,382:** • Use an odd number of oblique stripes to decorate the tail.
10 Make bubbles.	**34,400:** • Set your compass for a 1-in.-diameter circle. • Draw an even number of circles coming out of the fish's mouth.	**3,440:** • Set your compass for a 1-in.-diameter circle. • Draw an odd number of circles coming out of the fish's mouth.

Follow-the-Directions Solve & Draw Math, Grades 6–8 • © 2009 by Merideth Anderson • Scholastic Teaching Resources

Step/Question	If your answer is . . .	
(11) Decorate the body. or	**35,002:** • Shade every other stripe you drew in step 8.	**9,460:** • Draw horizontal stripes in every other stripe you drew in step 8.
(12) Decorate the body. or	**31,164:** • Fill with dots the remaining stripes you drew in step 8.	**4,452:** • Draw horizontal stripes in the remaining stripes you drew in step 8.
(13) Decorate the eye. or	**60 r5:** • Shade the circle you drew in step 7.	**66 r2:** • Draw horizontal stripes in the circle you drew in step 7.
(14) Decorate the tail. or	**75 r4:** • Polka-dot half the triangles you drew in step 9.	**705 r4:** • Make a pattern other than polka-dots in half the triangles you drew in step 9.
(15) Draw a fish hook.	**407 r11:** • Draw a fishing hook extending down at least 1½ in. from the top right-hand corner of the page.	**47 r11:** • Draw a fishing hook extending down at least 1½ in. from the top left-hand corner of the page.
(16) Add your final touches! or	**34 r21:** • Draw a smaller fish using the same shape as the big fish.	**340 r21:** • Draw a worm on the hook you drew in step 15.

School Bus Statistics

Materials

* School Bus Statistics: Solve It (page 13)
* School Bus Statistics: Hidden Picture Directions (pages 14–16)
* Protractor
* Ruler
* Compass
* Copy paper (11 x 17)
* Pencil

Vocabulary

Diameter: a segment passing through the center of a circle with its endpoints on the circle

Hexagon: a polygon with six sides

Horizontal: parallel to the horizon (left to right)

Oblique segment: a segment that is neither horizontal nor vertical

Rectangle: a parallelogram with four right angles

Segment: a part of a line with two endpoints

Semicircle: a half of a circle

Vertical: perpendicular to the horizon (up and down)

Getting Started

1. Hand out copies of School Bus Statistics: Solve It and have students answer the problems.

2. When students have completed the practice page, hand out School Bus Statistics: Hidden Picture Directions. Review the steps with students and complete one or two steps with them, reminding them to take their time and read through the steps carefully.

3. To begin the drawing, have students collect the materials listed at left and set their papers horizontally (landscape).

4. If students are unfamiliar with using a compass to draw circles and arcs, model the procedure on page 6 before students begin drawing their hidden picture. Step 7 requires the use of a compass.

5. If students are unfamiliar with using a protractor to draw angles, model the procedure on page 6 before students begin drawing their hidden picture. Step 5 requires the use of a protractor.

Solution to School Bus Statistics Hidden Drawing

Answers (page 13)

1. Mean: 86, Median: 85, Mode: 85

2. Mean: 74, Median: 74, Mode: No Mode

3. Mean: $2\frac{2}{5}$, Median: $2\frac{1}{2}$, Mode: 3

4. Mean: 135, Median: 130, Mode: 129

5. Mean: 92, Median: 94, Mode: No Mode

6. Mean: $57\frac{1}{6}$, Median: 55, Mode: No Mode

7. Mean: $116\frac{1}{7}$, Median: 117, Mode: 110 & 121

8. Mean: $43\frac{1}{2}$, Median: 46, Mode: 46

9. Mean: $65\frac{1}{3}$, Median: $58\frac{1}{2}$, Mode: 63

10. Mean: $25\frac{3}{8}$, Median: 33, Mode: 33

11. Mean: 8, Median: $7\frac{1}{2}$, Mode: No Mode

12. Mean: 73, Median: 70, Mode: 80

13. Mean: $50\frac{1}{3}$, Median: 46, Mode: 47

14. Mean: $15\frac{1}{2}$, Median: 16, Mode: No Mode

15. Mean: $97\frac{5}{8}$, Median: 98, Mode: 98

16. Mean: 120, Median: 119, Mode: 117

Name _____ Date _____

Directions: Find the mean, median, and mode for each item. Show remainders as fractions.

(1) 85, 91, 76, 85, 93	**(2)** 72, 76, 73, 74, 75	**(3)** 1, 2, 3, 2, 3, 3, 2, 3, 1, 4	**(4)** 129, 156, 118, 147, 131, 129
Mean: _____	Mean: _____	Mean: _____	Mean: _____
Median: _____	Median: _____	Median: _____	Median: _____
Mode: _____	Mode: _____	Mode: _____	Mode: _____
(5) 86, 87, 95, 96, 88, 94, 98	**(6)** 60, 57, 53, 78, 44, 51	**(7)** 110, 121, 110, 121, 115, 117, 119	**(8)** 46, 38, 22, 48, 61, 46
Mean: _____	Mean: _____	Mean: _____	Mean: _____
Median: _____	Median: _____	Median: _____	Median: _____
Mode: _____	Mode: _____	Mode: _____	Mode: _____
(9) 54, 63, 47, 114, 51, 63	**(10)** 33, 35, 0, 34, 33, 35, 33, 0	**(11)** 8, 6, 5, 9, 7, 13	**(12)** 80, 80, 70, 67, 68
Mean: _____	Mean: _____	Mean: _____	Mean: _____
Median: _____	Median: _____	Median: _____	Median: _____
Mode: _____	Mode: _____	Mode: _____	Mode: _____
(13) 100, 47, 45, 32, 31, 47	**(14)** 9, 19, 21, 13	**(15)** 98, 97, 98, 98, 97, 98, 98, 97	**(16)** 120, 112, 130, 128, 124, 117, 118, 117, 121, 113
Mean: _____	Mean: _____	Mean: _____	Mean: _____
Median: _____	Median: _____	Median: _____	Median: _____
Mode: _____	Mode: _____	Mode: _____	Mode: _____

Directions: Use your answers to School Bus Statistics: Solve It to choose an answer for each step below. One step at a time, follow the directions to reveal the hidden picture!

Step/Question	If your answer is . . .	
1 Make the body of the bus.	**Mean = 86:** • In the center of your paper, draw a rectangle with a base of 15½ in. and a height of 7 in.	**Mean = 85:** • In the center of your paper, draw a rectangle with a base of 12 in. and a height of 5 in.
2 Make a wheel well.	**Median = 73:** • Starting from the bottom left corner of the rectangle, measure to the right and make a mark at 4 in. and another at 5½ in. • Use the segment between these marks as the bottom of a trapezoid. The other three sides should measure ½ in. • Erase the bottom of the trapezoid.	**Median = 74:** • Starting from the bottom left corner of the rectangle, measure to the right and make a mark at 4 in. and another at 6⅔ in. • Use the segment between the marks as the bottom of a trapezoid. The other three sides should measure 1½ in. • Erase the bottom of the trapezoid.
3 Make a wheel well.	**Mode = 3:** • Starting from the bottom right corner of the rectangle, measure to the left and make a mark at 2 in. and another at 4¾ in. • Use the segment between the marks as the bottom of a trapezoid. The other three sides should measure 1½ in. • Erase the bottom of the trapezoid.	**Mode = 2:** • Starting from the bottom right corner of the rectangle from step 1, measure over to the left and make a mark at 2 in. and another at 3½ in. • Use the segment between the marks as the bottom of a trapezoid. The other three sides should measure ½ in. • Erase the bottom of the trapezoid.
4 Make the front.	**Mean = 135:** • Draw a 6½-in. vertical segment moving up from the bottom left corner of the first trapezoid (step 2).	**Mean = 130:** • Draw a 5-in. vertical segment moving up from the bottom left corner of the first trapezoid (step 2).
5 Make the front.	**Median = 94:** • Place your pencil on the top endpoint of the segment you drew in step 4. • Use this point as the vertex to make a 140° angle, drawing a ½-in. oblique segment moving up and left.	**Median = 96:** • Place your pencil on the top endpoint of the segment you drew in step 4. • Use this point as the vertex to make a 140° angle, drawing a 2-in. oblique segment moving up and left.

Follow-the-Directions Solve & Draw Math, Grades 6–8 • © 2009 by Merideth Anderson • Scholastic Teaching Resources

Step/Question	If your answer is . . .	
6 Make the front.	**Mode = 0:** • Place your pencil in the top left corner of the rectangle from step 1. • Using your compass, round off this corner with a small semi-circle.	**No mode:** • Place your pencil in the top left corner of the rectangle from step 1. • Make two marks from this point, one ½ in. down and the other ½ in. to the right. • Erase the angle between the two marks and connect the endpoints.
7 Make the wheels.	**Mean = 116½:** • Set your compass for a 2-in. circle. • Draw a circle in each of the wheel wells (steps 2 and 3). Add a smaller circle inside each.	**Mean = 116:** • Set your compass for a 3-in. circle. • Draw a circle in each of the wheel wells (steps 2 and 3). Add a smaller circle inside each.
8 Make the windshield.	**Median = 46:** • Place your pencil on the top end-point of the segment you drew in step 6 and measure down 1 in. • Use this point as the top left corner of a rectangle with a base of 3 in. and height of 2 in.	**No median:** • Place your pencil on the top end-point of the segment you drew in step 6 and measure right 1 in. then down ½ in. • Use this point as the top left corner of a rectangle with a base of 4 in. and height of 3 in.
9 Make the headlights.	**No mode:** • Draw a perfect 1-in. hexagon. Set it ½ in. below the bottom left corner of the rectangle you drew in step 8. • Repeat this step ½ in. below the bottom right corner of the rectangle.	**Mode = 63:** • Draw a perfect ¼-in. hexagon. Set it ½ in. below the bottom left corner of the rectangle you drew in step 8. • Repeat this step ½ in. below the bottom right corner of the rectangle.
10 Make the grill.	**Mean = 25⅝:** • Draw a rectangle with a base of 2½ in. and a height of 1 in. Center this rectangle below the rectangle from step 8.	**Mean = 203:** • Draw a 2-in. square. Center this square below the rectangle from step 8.
11 Finish the grill.	**Median = 7½:** • Draw three horizontal segments, splitting the rectangle from step 10 into four equivalent sections.	**Median = 7 and 8:** • Draw two horizontal segments, splitting the rectangle from step 10 into three equivalent sections.

Step/Question	If your answer is . . .	
(12) Make the turn signals.	**Mode = 80:** • Draw a rectangle with a base of ½ in. and height of ¼ in. Set it ½ in. below the bottom left corner of the rectangle you drew in step 10. • Repeat this step ½ in. below the bottom right corner of the rectangle.	**Mode = 73:** • Draw a 1-in. square. Set it ½ in. below the bottom left corner of the rectangle from step 10. • Repeat this step ½ in. below the bottom right corner of the rectangle.
(13) Make the door.	**Mean = 50⅓:** • Draw a rectangle with a base of 2 in. and height of 5 ½ in. Center it between the wheel wells.	**Mean = 46:** • Draw a 4-in. square. Center it between the wheel wells.
(14) Make the windows.	**Median = 16:** • Draw three 2-in. squares, one to the left of the door (step 13) and two to the right.	**Median = 19 and 21:** • Draw four 2-in. squares, two on each side of the door (step 13).
(15) Make the bumper.	**No mode:** • Place your pencil on the bottom left corner of the rectangle you drew in step 1. • Measure up 1 in. and make a mark. • Draw a horizontal segment connecting the mark you just made to the segment you drew in step 4. • Shade the rectangle you just drew.	**Mode = 98:** • Place your pencil on the bottom left corner of the rectangle you drew in step 1. • Measure up ½ in. and make a mark. • Draw a horizontal segment connecting the mark you just made to the segment from step 4. • Shade the rectangle you just drew.
(16) Make the steering wheel.	**Mean = 119:** • In the bottom right corner of the rectangle from step 8 draw the top half of a perfect 1-in. hexagon.	**Mean = 120:** • Set your compass for a circle smaller than 2 in. • In the bottom right corner of the rectangle from step 8, draw a semicircle. • Draw a second, smaller semicircle inside the first.

Follow-the-Directions Solve & Draw Math, Grades 6–8 • © 2009 by Merideth Anderson • Scholastic Teaching Resources

Batty 'Bout Decimals

Materials

✱ Batty 'Bout Decimals: Solve It (page 18)
✱ Batty 'Bout Decimals: Hidden Picture Directions (pages 19–21)
✱ Ruler
✱ Compass
✱ Copy paper (8½ x 14 or larger)
✱ Pencil

Vocabulary

Diameter: a segment passing through the center of a circle with its endpoints on the circle

Equilateral triangle: a triangle with three equal sides

Horizontal: parallel to the horizon (left to right)

Isosceles triangle: a triangle with exactly two equal sides

Parallel segments: segments that lie in the same plane but never intersect

Reflection: a mirror image over a given point

Getting Started

1. Hand out copies of Batty 'Bout Decimals: Solve It and have students answer the problems.

2. When students have completed the practice page, hand out the Batty 'Bout Decimals: Hidden Picture Directions pages. Review the steps with students and complete one or two steps with them, reminding them to take their time and read through the steps carefully.

3. To begin the drawing, have students collect the materials listed at left and set their papers horizontally (landscape).

4. If students are unfamiliar with using a compass to draw circles and arcs, model the procedure on page 6 before students begin drawing their hidden picture. Steps 1, 6, 7, and 14 require the use of a compass.

5. As you assist students, keep in mind that equilateral triangles have three 60° angles, which will help in drawing the wings (steps 3 and 4). Also, the diameter drawn in step 2 needs to be drawn lightly, as students will erase it.

Solution to Batty 'Bout Decimals Hidden Drawing

Answers (page 18)

1. seven thousand eight hundred ninety-two ten thousandths
2. one and five hundred ninety-nine ten thousandths
3. fourteen and seven hundred eighty-six thousandths
4. two hundred fifty-seven and one thousand fifty-two ten thousandths
5. thirteen and eight hundredths
6. two and two hundred seventy-five thousandths
7. two hundred sixty-five thousandths
8. eighty-nine and three hundredths
9. 0.0031
10. 5.0789
11. 50.011
12. 1,038.85
13. 0.478
14. 0.08
15. 61.0004
16. 0.9

Name _____ Date _____

Directions: Write the decimals in words or digits.

Write the decimals in words.

1 0.7892 _____

2 1.0599 _____

3 14.7860 _____

4 257.1052 _____

5 13.08 _____

6 2.2750 _____

7 0.265 _____

8 89.03 _____

Write the decimals in standard form.

9 thirty-one ten thousandths _____

10 five and seven hundred eighty-nine ten thousandths _____

11 fifty and eleven thousandths _____

12 one thousand, thirty-eight and eighty-five hundredths _____

13 four hundred seventy-eight thousandths _____

14 eight hundredths _____

15 sixty-one and forty hundred thousandths _____

16 ninety hundredths _____

Follow-the-Directions Solve & Draw Math, Grades 6–8 • © 2009 by Merideth Anderson • Scholastic Teaching Resources

Directions: Use your answers to the Batty 'Bout Decimals: Solve It to choose an answer for each step below. One step at a time, follow the directions to reveal the hidden picture.

Step/Question	If your answer is . . .	
1 Draw the body.	**seven thousand eight hundred ninety-two ten thousandths:** • Set your compass for a 3-in. circle and draw a circle in the center of the page.	**seven thousand eight hundred ninety-two thousandths:** • Set your compass for a 6-in. circle and draw a circle in the center of the page.
2 Draw the wings.	**one and five hundred ninety-nine hundredths:** • Place your pencil on the center point of the circle (step 1). • Draw the vertical diameter, lightly. • Extend the diameter out 4 in. in both directions of the circle.	**one and five hundred ninety-nine ten thousandths:** • Place your pencil on the center point of the circle (step 1). • Draw the horizontal diameter, lightly. • Extend the diameter out 4 in. in both directions of the circle.
3 Draw the wings.	**fourteen point seven hundred eighty-six ten thousandths:** • Place your pencil on the left endpoint of the segment from step 2. • Draw four 1-in. equilateral triangles, using the segment as a base. • Repeat this step on the right side of the circle (step 1).	**fourteen and seven hundred eighty-six thousandths:** • Place your pencil on the left endpoint of the segment from step 2. • Draw two 2-in. equilateral triangles using the segment as a base. • Repeat this step on the right side of the circle (step 1).
4 Draw the wings.	**two hundred fifty-seven and one thousand fifty-two ten thousandths:** • Use the segment from step 2 as a line of reflection. Reflect the triangles you just drew below the segment from step 2. • Erase the segment, including the diameter, you drew in step 2.	**two hundred fifty-seven and one thousand fifty-two ten thousands:** • Slide the triangles you just drew below the segment from step 2. • Erase the segment, including the diameter, you drew in step 2.
5 Make the ears.	**thirteen and eight hundredths:** • Draw two isosceles triangles with a ½-in. base and 1-in. sides. Set them side by side and centered on top of the circle (step 1).	**thirteen and eight tenths:** • Draw two equilateral triangles with 1-in. sides. Set them side by side and centered on top of the circle (step 1).

Step/Question	If your answer is . . .	
6 Make the eyes.	**two point two, seven, five, zero:** • Set your compass for a 1-in.-diameter circle. • Draw two circles side by side in the top half of the circle you drew in step 1.	**two and two hundred seventy-five thousandths:** • Set your compass for a ½-in.-diameter circle. • Draw two circles side by side in the top half of the circle you drew in step 1.
7 Make the nose.	**two hundred sixty-five thousandths:** • Set your compass for a ½-in.-diameter circle. • Draw a circle centered below and between the eyes.	**two hundred sixty-five thousands:** • Set your compass for a 1-in.-diameter circle. • Draw a circle centered below and between the eyes.
8 Make the mouth.	**eighty-nine and three hundredths:** • Make a mouth in any shape below the nose. • Draw two isosceles triangles as teeth. The two equal sides should measure more than 1 in.	**eighty-nine and three tenths:** • Make a mouth in any shape below the nose. • Draw two equilateral triangles as teeth with 1-in. sides.
9 Make the legs.	**0.0031:** • Draw two pairs of ½-in. vertical parallel segments down from the bottom of the body circle (step 1).	**0.0310:** • Draw four pairs of ¼-in. vertical parallel segments down from the bottom of the body circle (step 1).
10 Make the claws.	**5.0789:** • Add an odd number of claws connecting each pair of parallel segments.	**5.7089:** • Add an even number of claws connecting each pair of parallel segments.
11 Decorate the wings.	**50.011:** • Draw any pattern you wish in the triangles you drew in steps 3 and 4.	**50.0011:** • Shade the triangles you drew in steps 3 and 4.

Follow-the-Directions Solve & Draw Math, Grades 6–8 • © 2009 by Merideth Anderson • Scholastic Teaching Resources

Step/Question	If your answer is . . .	
12 Decorate the body.	**1,380.85:** • Draw vertical stripes in the circle you drew in step 1 (do not include the eyes, nose, mouth, or teeth).	**1,038.85:** • Shade the circle you drew in step 1 (do not include the eyes, nose, mouth, or teeth).
13 Decorate the ears and feet.	**0.478:** • Draw any pattern you wish in the ears you drew in step 5. • Draw the same pattern in the feet and claws you drew in steps 9 and 10.	**0.0478:** • Shade the ears you drew in step 5. • Shade the feet and claws you drew in steps 9 and 10.
14 Make a moon.	**0.008:** • Set your compass for a 3-in.-diameter circle. • Draw a circle in the upper left-hand portion of the page.	**0.08:** • Set your compass for a 7-in.-diameter circle. • Place the sharp tip of the compass on the center point of the circle you drew in step 1, and draw a circle.
15 Make clouds.	**61.0004:** • Draw an even number of clouds in the background.	**61.004:** • Draw an odd number of clouds in the background.
16 Decorate the clouds.	**0.09:** • Draw any pattern you wish in the clouds.	**0.9:** • Shade the clouds.

Fine Feathered Equations

Materials

* Fine Feathered Equations: Solve It (page 23)
* Fine Feathered Equations: Hidden Picture Directions (pages 24–26)
* Ruler
* Compass
* Copy paper (8½ x 14 or larger)
* Pencil

Vocabulary

Diameter: a segment passing through the center of a circle with its endpoints on the circle

Equilateral triangle: a triangle with three equal sides

Isosceles triangle: a triangle with exactly two equal sides

Oblique segment: a segment that is neither vertical nor horizontal

Parallel segments: segments that lie in the same plane but never intersect

Segment: a part of a line with two endpoints

Semicircle: a half of a circle

Square: a parallelogram with four right angles and four equal sides

Vertical: perpendicular to the horizon (up and down)

Getting Started

1. Hand out copies of Fine Feathered Equations: Solve It and have students answer the problems.

2. When students have completed the practice page, hand out Fine Feathered Equations: Hidden Picture Directions. Review the steps with students and complete one or two steps with them, reminding them to take their time and read through the steps carefully.

3. To begin the drawing, have students collect the materials listed at left and set their papers horizontally (landscape).

4. If students are unfamiliar with using a compass to draw circles and arcs, model the procedure on page 6 before students begin drawing their hidden picture. Steps 1, 2, and 9 require the use of a compass.

5. As you assist students, keep in mind the following: the circles drawn in steps 1 and 2 share their bottom arc in common; steps 5 through 8 involve forming the plume of the turkey, and students should spread out the segments in step 7 evenly; the claws (step 11) can take any shape but must use six segments per foot.

Solution to Fine Feathered Equations Hidden Drawing

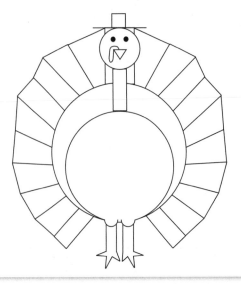

Answers (page 23)

1. 4	**9.** -140
2. -3	**10.** 13
3. 121	**11.** ½
4. -2	**12.** 7⅓
5. 35	**13.** 19½
6. 1⅔	**14.** 12
7. -15	**15.** 0
8. -56	**16.** 248

Name _____ Date _____

Directions: Solve each problem. Remember to reduce the fractions and show your work.

1 $5d - 8 = 12$	**2** $8r - 8 = -32$

3 $\dfrac{m}{-11} + 1 = -10$	**4** $-5h - 2 = 8$

5 $\dfrac{x}{-7} + 3 = -2$	**6** $-3a + 17 = 12$

7 $-2y - 10 = 20$	**8** $\dfrac{b}{-8} - 4 = 3$

9 $\dfrac{m}{-10} - 5 = 9$	**10** $-118 = 12 - 10x$

11 $7 + 13m = 13.5$	**12** $3d - 5 = 17$

13 $4n - 6 = 72$	**14** $\dfrac{w}{2} - 7 = -1$

15 $\dfrac{x}{3} - 15 = -15$	**16** $\dfrac{-x}{4} + 8 = -54$

Directions: Use your answers to Fine Feathered Friends: Solve It to choose an answer for each step below. One step at a time, follow the directions to reveal the hidden picture.

Step/Question	If your answer is . . .	
1 Make the body. 	**100:** • Set your compass for a 6-in.-diameter circle. • Draw the circle in the center of the page.	**4:** • Set your compass for a 4-in.-diameter circle. • Draw the circle in the center of the page.
2 Make the body. 	**-3:** • Set your compass for a 5-in.-diameter circle. • Draw a circle around the outside of the circle you drew in step 1. • Draw the second circle so that it shares the bottom arc of the first circle.	**-5:** • Draw a 7-in. square around the outside of the circle you drew in step 1. • Draw the square so the bottom side meets the lowest point of the circle.
3 Make the neck. 	**99:** • On top of the body, draw a cylinder with a base of ½ in. and a height of 1½ in. Set the base on the top center point on the circle you drew in step 1.	**121:** • On top of the body, draw a rectangle with a base of ½ in. and height of 1½ in. Set the base on the top center point on the circle you drew in step 1.
4 Make the head. 	**2:** • Set your compass for a 3-in.-diameter circle. • Draw a circle centered on top of the neck you drew in step 3.	**-2:** • Set your compass for a 1½-in.-diameter circle. • Draw a circle centered on top of the neck you drew in step 3.
5 Make the feathers. 	**35:** • Draw two 2-in. vertical segments. Start from the top of the body (step 2) and center the head (step 4) between the segments. • Connect the tops of these segments with a shorter segment.	**-7:** • Draw two 1-in. vertical segments. Start from the top of the body (step 2) and center the head (step 4) between the segments. • Connect the tops of these segments with a shorter segment.

Follow-the-Directions Solve & Draw Math, Grades 6–8 • © 2009 by Merideth Anderson • Scholastic Teaching Resources

Step/Question	If your answer is . . .	
6 Make the feathers. 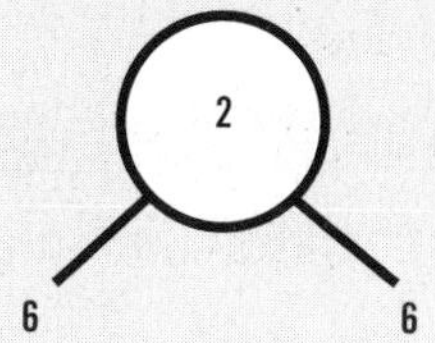 (circle labeled 2, with segments labeled 6, 6)	**1⅔:** • From the bottom center of the outer circle (step 2), move your pencil around the circle about 2 in. • Draw a 1½-in. oblique line segment extending out. • Repeat this step moving in the opposite direction from the bottom center of the circle.	**15:** • From the bottom center of the outer circle (step 2), move your pencil around the circle about 1¼ in. • Draw a ¾-in. oblique line segment extending out. • Repeat this step moving in the opposite direction from the bottom center of the circle.
7 Make the feathers.  (circle labeled 2 with segments labeled 5, 7s, 6)	**5:** • Draw 8 segments, between 2 in. and 4 in. long, extending out from the outer circle (step 2). • Five segments should be drawn on the right half of the circle and five on the left half of the circle.	**-15:** • Draw 18 segments, between ¾ in. and 2 in. long, extending out from the outer circle (step 2). • Nine segments should be drawn on the right half of the circle and nine on the left half of the circle.
8 Make the feathers.  (shapes labeled 8, 7 or 8, 7, 7) 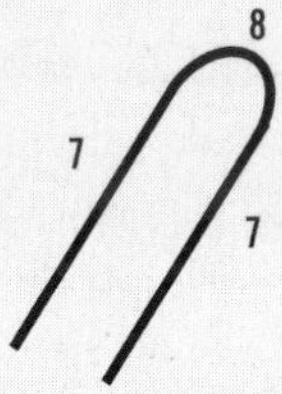	**-56:** • Connect the ends of the segments you drew in steps 6 and 7 with segments. Do not connect the bottom two segments. • You will use a total of 20 segments.	**-⅞:** • Connect the ends of the segments coming from the circle you drew in steps 6 and 7 with arcs. Do not connect the bottom two segments. • You will use a total of 20 arcs.
9 Make the legs.  (circle labeled 1 with 9 below)	**-140:** • Set your compass for a ½-in.-diameter circle. • Draw two semicircles attached to the bottom of the circle you drew in step 1, leaving ¼ in. between the two semicircles.	**-1⅖:** • Set your compass for a 1-in.-diameter circle. • Draw two semicircles attached to the bottom of the circle you drew in step 1, leaving ¼ in. between the two semicircles.
10 Make the legs. 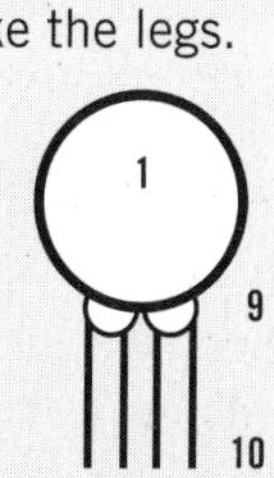 (circle labeled 1 with 9, 10)	**13:** • Draw a pair of 1-in. parallel, vertical line segments extending down from the bottom of each semicircle you drew in step 9. • Set these segments at least ¼ in. apart.	**10⅗:** • Draw a pair of 4-in. parallel, vertical line segments extending down from the bottom of each semicircle you drew in step 9. • Set these segments at least ¼ in. apart.
11 Make the claws.  (claw shapes: or) 	**½:** • Between each pair of segments you drew in step 10, draw six line segments to form claws.	**1¹⁵⁄₂₆:** • Between each pair of segments you drew in step 10, draw 10 line segments to form claws.

Step/Question	If your answer is . . .	
12 Make a hat. 12 (4)	**4:** • Draw a 2-in. horizontal line segment centered on top of the circle you drew in step 4.	**7⅓:** • Draw a 1¼-in. horizontal line segment centered on top of the circle you drew in step 4.
13 Make a hat. □ or △	**19½:** • Draw a ½-in. square centered on top of the segment you drew in step 12.	**-4½:** • Draw a ½-in. equilateral triangle centered on top of the segment you drew in step 12.
14 Make the beak. ▽ or ▽	**3:** • In the center of the circle you drew in step 4, draw an equilateral triangle with the sides measuring ¾ in. and the tip pointing down.	**12:** • In the center of the circle you drew in step 4, draw an isosceles triangle with the top measuring ½ in., the sides ⅜ in., and the tip pointing down.
15 Make the eyes. ♥ or ●	**-10:** • Draw two dark hearts horizontally above the triangle you drew in step 14.	**0:** • Draw two dark points horizontally above the triangle you drew in step 14.
16 Draw the snood. (4) 16 14	**248:** • Draw a snood connecting to the base of the triangle you drew in step 14.	**15½:** • Draw a snood connecting to the bottom of the circle you drew in step 4.

Follow-the-Directions Solve & Draw Math, Grades 6–8 • © 2009 by Merideth Anderson • Scholastic Teaching Resources

Rounding Skills to Crow About

Materials

* Rounding Skills to Crow About: Solve It (page 28)
* Rounding Skills to Crow About: Hidden Picture Directions (pages 29–31)
* Ruler
* Compass
* Copy paper (8½ x 14 or larger)
* Pencil

Vocabulary

Arc: a part of a circle

Diameter: a segment passing through the center of a circle with its endpoints on the circle

Equilateral triangle: a triangle with three equal sides

Horizontal: parallel to the horizon (left to right)

Parallel segments: segments that lie in the same plane but never intersect

Quadrilateral: a four-sided polygon

Rectangle: a parallelogram with four right angles

Segment: a part of a line with two endpoints

Trapezium: a quadrilateral with no pairs of parallel sides

Vertical: perpendicular to the horizon (up and down)

Getting Started

1. Hand out copies of Rounding Skills to Crow About: Solve It and have students answer the problems.

2. When students have completed the practice page, hand out Rounding Skills to Crow About: Hidden Picture Directions. Review the steps with students and complete one or two steps with them, reminding them to take their time and read through the steps carefully.

3. To begin the drawing, have students collect the materials listed at left and set their papers vertically (portrait).

4. If students are unfamiliar with using a compass to draw circles and arcs, model the procedure on page 6 before students begin drawing their hidden picture. Steps 3, 8, 11, and 14 require the use of a compass.

5. As you assist students, remind them to do the following: center the vertical segment (step 1); make sure the trapeziums (steps 6 and 7) stretch across the entire bottom of the rectangle (step 5); after step 5, erase all the segments inside the rectangles (steps 4 and 5) to form a shirt.

Fast Finishers

Have students who finish early write a journal article placing themselves in the shoes of a scarecrow. Have them describe the farm or garden they're watching over, noting plants, animals, and people in the scene. To challenge them, have students include some of the following vocabulary words: *arc, line segment, horizontal line segment, vertical line segment, parallel, isosceles triangle, diameter, trapezium, quadrilateral, equilateral triangle, rectangle.*

Solution to Rounding Skills to Crow About Hidden Drawing

Answers (page 28)

1. 4,600	**6.** 16.78	**11.** 100.0
2. 10,000	**7.** 30	**12.** 615.35
3. 36,000	**8.** 1.0	**13.** 140
4. 325	**9.** 36.47	**14.** 88,000
5. 30	**10.** 16,000,000	**15.** 13.2

Name _____ Date _____

Directions: Round each decimal to the underlined digit.

1 4,5̲72	**2** 9,9̲87	**3** 36̲,421
4 324̲.6	**5** 2̲5.982	**6** 16.78̲3
7 2̲7.593	**8** 0.9̲78	**9** 36.47̲3
10 15̲,968,213	**11** 99.9̲99	**12** 615.34̲5
13 13̲5.124	**14** 87̲,796	**15** 13.1̲6589

Follow-the-Directions Solve & Draw Math, Grades 6–8 • © 2009 by Merideth Anderson • Scholastic Teaching Resources

Rounding Skills to Crow About: Hidden Picture Directions

Directions: Use your answers to Rounding Skills to Crow About: Solve It to choose an answer for each step below. One step at a time, follow the directions to reveal the hidden picture.

Step/Question	If your answer is . . .	
1 Make a post.	**4,600:** • In the center of the page, draw a 5-in. vertical segment.	**4,672:** • In the center of the page, draw a 3-in. vertical segment.
2 Finish the post.	**10,000:** • From the top of the segment you drew in step 1, measure down ½ in. and make a mark. • Draw a 4-in. horizontal segment. Center the segment by extending it 2 in. on each side of the vertical line.	**9,900:** • From the top of the segment you drew in step 1, draw a 4-in. horizontal segment. Center the segment by extending it 2 in. on each side of the vertical line.
3 Make the head.	**37,000:** • Set your compass for a 5-in.-diameter circle. • Draw a circle connected to the top of the vertical line you drew in step 1.	**36,000:** • Set your compass for a 3-in.-diameter circle. • Draw a circle connected to the top of the vertical line you drew in step 1.
4 Make the shirt.	**325.6:** • From the top of the segment you drew in step 1, measure down 2½ in. • Using this point as the top center of the rectangle, draw a rectangle 3 in. wide and 1¼ in. high.	**325:** • From the top of the segment you drew in step 1, measure down ¼ in. • Using this point as the top center of the rectangle, draw a rectangle 3-in. wide and 1¼ in. high.
5 Make the shirt.	**30:** • Centered on the bottom of the rectangle you drew in step 4, draw a rectangle 1½ in. wide and 2 in. tall. • Erase all the lines inside the two rectangles you drew in steps 4 and 5. Erase the top line of the rectangle and the vertical line you drew in step 1.	**30.982:** • Set your compass for a 3-in.-diameter circle. • Draw a circle connected to the bottom of the rectangle you drew in step 4. • Inside the shapes you drew in steps 4 and 5, erase the vertical line you drew in step 1.

Step/Question	If your answer is . . .	
(6) Make the legs.	**16.78:** • Starting from the bottom left corner of the rectangle you drew in step 5, draw a trapezium with the top measuring ¾ in., the bottom 1 in., the left side 2½ in., and the right side 3 in. • The top of the trapezium should run along the bottom left side of the rectangle (step 5).	**16.79:** • Starting from the bottom left corner of the rectangle you drew in step 5, draw a trapezium with the top measuring 2½ in., the bottom 3 in., the left side ¾ in., and the right side 1 in. • The top of the trapezium should run along the bottom of the rectangle (step 5).
(7) Make the legs.	**30.593:** • Starting from the bottom right corner of the rectangle you drew in step 5, draw a trapezium with the top measuring 2½ in., the bottom 3 in., the left side ¾ in., and the right side 1 in. • The top of the trapezium should run along the bottom right side of the rectangle (step 5).	**30:** • Starting from the bottom right corner of the rectangle you drew in step 5, draw a trapezium with the top measuring ¾ in., the bottom 1 in., the left side 3 in., and the right side 2½ in. • The top of the trapezium should run along the bottom right side of the rectangle (step 5).
(8) Make the eyes.	**0.10:** • Draw two ½-in. squares side by side in the top half of the circle you drew in step 3.	**1.0:** • Set your compass for a ½-in. diameter circle. • Draw two circles side by side in the top half of the circle you drew in step 3.
(9) Make the nose.	**36.47:** • Draw an equilateral triangle with ½-in. sides centered below and between the eyes you drew in step 8.	**36.5:** • Set your compass for a ½-in. circle. • Draw a circle centered below and between the eyes you drew in step 8.
(10) Make the mouth. **X**	**16,968,213:** • Draw an even number of x's in an arc near the bottom of the circle you drew in step 3.	**16,000,000:** • Draw an odd number of x's in an arc shape near the bottom of the circle you drew in step 3.
(11) Make the hands.	**100.000:** • Draw a ½-in. square connected to each end of the horizontal segment you drew in step 2.	**100.0:** • Set your compass for a ½-in. diameter circle. • Draw a circle connected to each end of the horizontal segment you drew in step 2.

Step/Question	If your answer is . . .	
(12) Make a hat.	**615.34:** • At the top of the circle you drew in step 3, draw an isosceles triangle, the bottom side measuring 2 in. and the other two sides measuring 3 in.	**615.35:** • Centered on top of the circle you drew in step 3, draw a 2-in. horizontal segment.
(13) Make a hat.	**140:** • Centered on top of the segment you drew in step 12, draw a square with 1-in. sides.	**140.124:** • Centered on top of the segment you drew in step 12, draw a square with 2-in. sides.
(14) Make the feet.	**87,000:** • Set your compass for a ½-in.-diameter circle. • Draw a circle connected to the bottom of each trapezium you drew in steps 6 and 7.	**88,000:** • Set your compass for a 1-in.-diameter circle. • Draw a circle connected to the bottom of each trapezium you drew in steps 6 and 7.
(15) Final touches.	**13.26589:** • Draw a crow sitting on top of the hat you drew in step 13.	**13.2:** • Draw straw coming out of the legs you drew in steps 6 and 7, the sleeves of the shirt you drew in step 4, and under the hat you drew in steps 12 and 13.

Coordinated Crocodile

Materials

* Coordinated Crocodile: Solve It (page 33)
* Coordinated Crocodile: Hidden Picture Directions (pages 34–36)
* Ruler
* Compass
* Protractor
* Copy paper (11 x 17)
* Pencil

Vocabulary

Diameter: a segment passing through the center of a circle with its endpoints on the circle

Horizontal: parallel to the horizon (left to right)

Line segment: a part of a line with two endpoints

Oblique: a segment that is neither vertical nor horizontal

Parallel segments: segments that lie on the same plane and never intersect

Rectangle: a parallelogram with four right angles

Vertical: perpendicular to the horizon (up and down)

Getting Started

1. Hand out copies of Coordinated Crocodile: Solve It and have students answer the problems.

2. When students have completed the practice page, hand out Coordinated Crocodile: Hidden Picture Directions. Review the steps with students and complete one or two steps with them. Remind them to take their time and read through the answer options for each step carefully.

3. To begin the drawing, have students collect the materials listed at left and set their papers horizontally (landscape).

4. If students are unfamiliar with using a compass to draw circles and arcs, model the procedure on page 6 before students begin drawing their hidden picture. Step 10 requires students to use a compass.

5. If students are unfamiliar with using a protractor to draw angles, model the procedure on page 6 before students begin drawing their hidden picture. In steps 2–8, students must use a protractor.

6. As you assist students, remind them that the triangles on the tail and back (steps 8 and 9) can be any size, as can the triangles in steps 14 and 16.

⚡ Fast Finishers

Have students who finish early complete the following story starter: "There once was a great big crocodile . . . ." To challenge students have them include some of the following vocabulary words: *Oblique, line segment, horizontal, vertical, parallel segment, rectangle.*

Answers (page 33)

1. Quadrant 3	9. X-Axis
2. Quadrant 2	10. Quadrant 3
3. Quadrant 4	11. Quadrant 1
4. Quadrant 1	12. Quadrant 4
5. Quadrant 2	13. Quadrant 2
6. Quadrant 4	14. Y-Axis
7. Y-Axis	15. X-Axis
8. Quadrant 3	16. Origin

Solution to Coordinated Crocodile Hidden Drawing

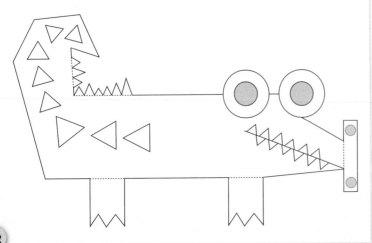

Name _____ Date _____

Directions: Graph each point and identify its location. Location options include: Quadrant I, Quadrant II, Quadrant III, Quadrant IV, X-axis, Y-axis, or Origin. Use your answers to create a picture with Coordinated Crocodile: Hidden Picture Directions page.

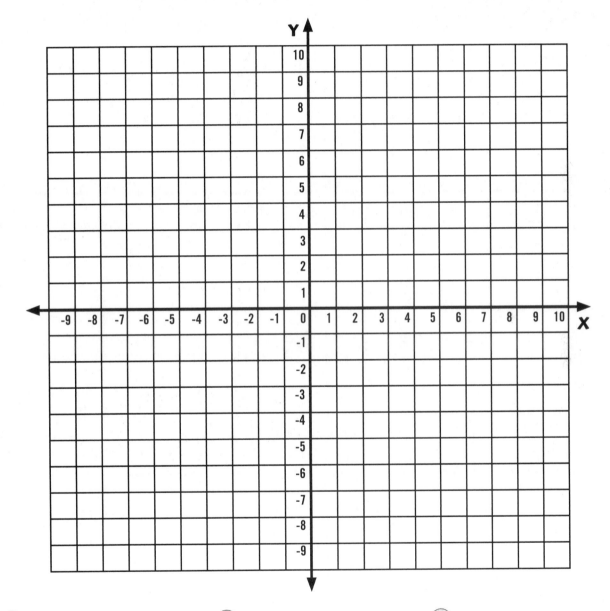

1 A (-2,-1) _____

2 B (-1,2) _____

3 C (1,-4) _____

4 D (6,4) _____

5 E (-3,4) _____

6 F (7,-1) _____

7 G (0,5) _____

8 H (-1,-3) _____

9 I (4,0) _____

10 J (-6,-5) _____

11 K (2,1) _____

12 L (3,-4) _____

13 M (-5,6) _____

14 N (0,2) _____

15 O (7,0) _____

16 P (0,0) _____

Directions: Use your answers to Coordinated Crocodile: Solve It to choose an answer for each step below. One step at a time, follow the directions to reveal the hidden picture.

Step/Question	If your answer is . . .	
1 Make the body. ——————————— 1	**Quadrant 3:** • From the bottom left corner of the page, measure up 3¾ in. and then right 3 in. Make a mark. • From this point, draw a 9¼-in. horizontal line segment to the right.	**Quadrant 4:** • From the center of the page, draw an 8-in. horizontal line segment, extending left.
2 Make the body. (diagram with 2) 1 **or** (diagram) 1 — 2	**Quadrant 4:** • Place your pencil on the right endpoint of the segment you drew in step 1. • Draw a 2-in. vertical segment extending up.	**Quadrant 2:** • Use the segment you drew in step 1 as a base and its right endpoint as a vertex. Measure a 174° angle, drawing a 3¾-in. oblique line segment extending up and to the right.
3 Make the tail. 3 (diagram) 1	**Quadrant 4:** • Use the segment you drew in step 1 as a base and its left endpoint as a vertex. Measure a 110° angle, drawing a 4¾-in. oblique line segment extending up and to the left.	**Quadrant 1:** • Use the segment you drew in step 1 as a base and its left endpoint as a vertex. Measure a 110° angle, drawing a 2-in. oblique line segment extending up and to the left.
4 Make the tail. 4 (diagram) 3	**Quadrant 2:** • Use the segment you drew in step 3 as a base and its top endpoint as a vertex. Measure a 138° angle, drawing a 1-in. oblique segment extending up and to the right.	**Quadrant 1:** • Use the segment you drew in step 3 as a base and its top endpoint as a vertex. Measure a 138° angle, drawing a 2-in. oblique segment extending up and to the right.
5 Make the tail. 5 (diagram) 4	**Quadrant 2:** • Use the segment you drew in step 4 as a base and its top endpoint as a vertex. Measure a 125° angle, drawing a 1⅝-in. oblique line segment extending up and to the right.	**Quadrant 3:** • Use the segment you drew in step 4 as a base and its top endpoint as a vertex. Measure a 125° angle, drawing a 2-in. oblique line segment extending up and to the right.

Follow-the-Directions Solve & Draw Math, Grades 6–8 • © 2009 by Merideth Anderson • Scholastic Teaching Resources

Step/Question	If your answer is . . .	
6 Make the tail.	**Quadrant 2:** • Use the segment you drew in step 5 as a base and its top endpoint as a vertex. Measure a 125° angle, drawing a 3-in. oblique line segment extending down and to the right.	**Quadrant 4:** • Use the segment you drew in step 5 as a base and its top endpoint as a vertex. Measure a 109° angle, drawing a 2-in. oblique line segment extending down and to the right.
7 Make the tail.	**X-Axis:** • Use the segment you drew in step 6 as a base and its bottom endpoint as a vertex. Measure a 32° angle, drawing a 2½-in. oblique line segment extending up and to the left.	**Y-Axis:** • Use the segment you drew in step 6 as a base and its bottom endpoint as a vertex. Measure a 32° angle, drawing a 1½-in. oblique line segment extending up and to the left.
8 Make the tail.	**Quadrant 1:** • Use the segment you drew in step 7 as a base and its top endpoint as a vertex. Measure a 60° angle, drawing a 1-in. oblique line segment extending down and to the right. • On top of this segment draw three triangles pointing right. Erase the base of each triangle.	**Quadrant 3:** • Use the segment you drew in step 7 as a base and its top endpoint as a vertex. Measure a 60° angle, drawing a 3-in. oblique line segment extending down and to the right. • On top of this segment draw three triangles pointing right. Erase the base of each triangle.
9 Make the body.	**Origin:** • From the bottom endpoint of the segment you drew in step 8, draw a 5-in. horizontal segment to the right. • On the left half of this segment, draw six triangles. Erase the base of each triangle.	**X-Axis:** • From the bottom endpoint of the segment you drew in step 8, draw a 6¾-in. horizontal segment to the right. • On the left half of this segment, draw six triangles. Erase the base of each triangle.
10 Make the eyes.	**Quadrant 3:** • Set your compass for a 2-in.-diameter circle. • Draw two side-by-side circles: Connect one circle with the endpoint of the segment you drew in step 9 and set the other ⅜ in. directly to the right. Draw a line segment connecting these circles. • Draw and shade smaller circles inside each of the 2-in. circles.	**Quadrant 2:** • Set your compass for a 1-in.-diameter circle. • Draw two side-by-side circles: Connect one circle with the endpoint of the segment you drew in step 9 and set the other ⅜ in. directly to the right. Draw a line segment connecting these circles. • Draw and shade smaller circles inside each of the 1-in. circles.

Step/Question	If your answer is . . .	
11 Make the body.	**Quadrant 1:** • From the bottom of the right-hand circle you drew in step 10, draw a 3-in. oblique segment down and to the right. Make sure the bottom endpoint is directly above the right endpoint of the segment you drew in step 2.	**Quadrant 4:** From the bottom of the right-hand circle you drew in step 10, draw a 4-in. oblique segment down and to the right. Make sure the bottom endpoint is directly above the right endpoint of the segment you drew in step 2.
12 Make the snout.	**Quadrant 2:** • In the space between the right endpoints of the segments you drew in steps 2 and 11, draw a ¼-in.-by-2 ½-in. rectangle. • Erase the vertical segment on the left side.	**Quadrant 4:** • In the space between the right endpoints of the segments you drew in steps 2 and 11, draw a ¾-in.-by-3 ½-in. rectangle. • Erase the vertical segment on the left side.
13 Make a leg and claws.	**Quadrant 2:** • From the right endpoint of the segment you drew in step 1, draw a 2¼-in. vertical segment extending down. Draw a segment of equal length 1½-in. to the left and connect the bottoms with four short zigzag segments. • Erase the segment between the top endpoints.	**Quadrant 4:** • From the right endpoint of the segment you drew in step 1, draw a 1-in. vertical segment extending down. Draw a segment of equal length 1 in. to the left and connect the bottoms with four short zigzag segments. • Erase the segment between the top endpoints.
14 Make a leg and claws.	**X-Axis:** • From the top endpoint of the left-hand segment you drew in step 13, measure left 6½ in., and draw another leg as described in step 13.	**Y-Axis:** • From the top endpoint of the left-hand segment you drew in step 13, measure left 4½ in., and draw another leg as described in step 13.
15 Make the mouth.	**X-Axis:** • Use the segment you drew in step 2 as a base and its top endpoint as a vertex. Measure a 20° angle, drawing a 5½-in. oblique segment up and to the left. • Draw an even number of triangles above and below this segment.	**Y-Axis:** • Use the segment you drew in step 2 as a base and its top endpoint as a vertex. Measure a 20° angle, drawing a 2-in. oblique segment up and to the left. • Draw an even number of triangles above and below this segment.
16 Final touches: Nostrils and scales.	**Origin:** • Draw two large dots inside the rectangle you drew in step 12 (at the top and at the bottom). • Add an even number of shaded triangles inside the body.	**X-Axis:** • Draw two large dots inside the rectangle you drew in step 12 (at the top and at the bottom). • Add an odd number of shaded triangles inside the body.

Follow-the-Directions Solve & Draw Math, Grades 6–8 • © 2009 by Merideth Anderson • Scholastic Teaching Resources

Winter Numberland

Materials

* Winter Numberland: Solve It (page 38)
* Winter Numberland: Hidden Picture Directions (pages 39–40)
* Ruler
* Copy paper (8½ x 14 or larger)
* Pencil

Vocabulary

Decagon: a polygon with 10 sides

Diameter: a segment passing through the center of a circle with its endpoints on the circle

Scalene triangle: a triangle with no equal sides

Segment: a part of a line with two endpoints

Square: a parallelogram with four right angles and four equal sides

Trapezoid: a quadrilateral with exactly one pair of parallel sides

Getting Started

1. Hand out copies of Winter Numberland: Solve It and have students answer the problems.

2. When students have completed the practice page, hand out Winter Numberland: Hidden Picture Directions. Review the steps with students and complete one or two steps with them, reminding them to take their time and read through the steps carefully.

3. To begin the drawing, have students collect the materials listed at left and set their papers vertically (portrait).

4. When assisting students, have students start the star (step 6) by drawing the bottom two angles using the top point of the triangle (step 4).

⚡ Fast Finishers

Have students who finish early compose a creative story about the best winter day they can imagine. To challenge students, have them include some of the following vocabulary words: *trapezoid, scalene triangle, square, decagon, hexagon, octagon, segment.*

Solution to Winter Numberland Hidden Drawing

Answers (page 38)

1. 9.24	**9.** 23.3
2. 2.43	**10.** 7.82
3. 55.3	**11.** 1.479
4. 5.00	**12.** 6.0
5. 24.3	**13.** 22.3
6. 5.41	**14.** 3.10
7. 1,839.18	**15.** 0.00011
8. 3.5	**16.** 4

Name _____ Date _____

Directions: Solve each problem and show your work. Then round your answer.

1 3.086 + 6.152	**2** 3.4 − 0.972	**3** 9.87 × 5.6	**4** 73.05 ÷ 15
Round to the nearest hundredth: _____	Round to the nearest hundredth: _____	Round to the nearest tenth: _____	Round to the nearest whole number: _____
5 9.27 + 15.006	**6** 8.13 − 2.716	**7** 43.79 × 42	**8** 10.62 ÷ 3
Round to the nearest tenth: _____	Round to the nearest hundredth: _____	Round to the nearest hundredth: _____	Round to the nearest tenth: _____
9 14.05 + 9.2	**10** 14.75 − 6.9264	**11** 0.279 × 5.3	**12** 6.464 ÷ 1.01
Round to the nearest tenth: _____	Round to the nearest hundredth: _____	Round to the nearest thousandth: _____	Round to the nearest whole number: _____
13 9.104 + 5.2 + 7.99	**14** 5.9 − 2.803	**15** 0.019 × 0.0057	**16** 23.68 ÷ 6.4
Round to the nearest tenth: _____	Round to the nearest hundredth: _____	Round to the nearest hundred thousandth: _____	Round to the nearest whole number: _____

Follow-the-Directions Solve & Draw Math, Grades 6–8 • © 2009 by Merideth Anderson • Scholastic Teaching Resources

Directions: Use your answers to Winter Wonderland: Solve It to choose an answer for each step below. One step at a time, follow the directions to reveal the hidden picture.

Step/Question	If your answer is . . .	
(1) Make a tree.	**9.3:** • Measure up 4½ in. from the bottom of your page. • Draw a trapezoid with a 4-in. top, 2-in. sides, and a 5-in. bottom. • Center the figure between the sides of the page.	**9.24:** • Measure up 4½ in. from the bottom of your page. • Draw a trapezoid with a 6⅜-in top, 3-in. sides, and a 9-in. bottom. • Center the figure between the sides of the page.
(2) Make a tree.	**2.43:** • Draw a trapezoid with a 6-in. top, 3-in. sides, and an 8½-in. bottom. • Set the base of this trapezoid directly on top of the trapezoid you drew in step 1.	**2.438:** • Draw a trapezoid with an 8-in. top, 3-in. sides, and an 11-in. bottom. • Set the base of this trapezoid directly on top of the trapezoid you drew in step 1.
(3) Make a tree.	**55.3:** • Draw a trapezoid with a 5½-in. top, 3-in. sides, and an 8-in. bottom. • Set the base of this trapezoid directly on top of the trapezoid you drew in step 2.	**55.2:** • Draw a trapezoid with a 5-in. top, 4-in. sides, and a 6¼-in. bottom. • Set the base of this trapezoid directly on top of the trapezoid you drew in step 2.
(4) Make a tree.	**5.00:** • Directly on top of the trapezoid you drew in step 3, draw an equilateral triangle with 6-in. sides.	**4.00:** • Directly on top of the trapezoid you drew in step 3, draw a scalene triangle with a 8½-in. base, a 6-in. left side, and a 5¹³⁄₁₆-in. right side.
(5) Make the trunk of the tree.	**24.3:** • Centered directly beneath the trapezoid you drew in step 1, draw a 2-in. square.	**24.28:** • Centered directly beneath the trapezoid you drew in step 1, draw a 3-in. square.
(6) Finish the tree.	**5.41:** • On the top point of the triangle you drew in step 5, draw a concave decagon (commonly seen in the sky on a clear night). • All sides of your decagon should measure ¾ in.	**5.414:** • On the top point of the triangle you drew in step 5, draw a concave hexagon (commonly seen on a present). • All sides of your hexagon should measure ½ in.

Step/Question	If your answer is . . .	
(7) Make a bird. 	**1,839.2:** • On one side of the trapezoid you drew in step 1, draw a bird perched on the branches.	**1,839:18** • On one side of the trapezoid you drew in step 3, draw a bird perched on the branches.
(8) Add the background.  	**3.6:** • Draw the horizon in the middle of the page.	**3.5:** • Draw a hill in the background.
(9) Add a background.  	**23.3:** • Draw snowflakes in the background.	**23.25:** • Draw a rainbow in the background.
(10) Add a sun.  	**7.824:** • Set your compass for a 3½-in.-diameter circle. • At the top right-hand corner of the page, draw an arc.	**7.82:** • Set your compass for a 3½-in.-diameter circle. • At the top left-hand corner of the page, draw an arc.
(11) Add rays to the sun. 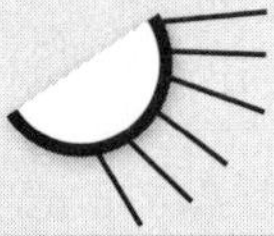	**1.4797:** • Draw an odd number of 1-in. rays coming from the sun you drew in step 10.	**1.479:** • Draw an even number of 1-in. rays coming from the sun you drew in step 10.
(12) Add children sledding. 	**6.0:** • Add an odd number of children to the hill you drew in step 8.	**7.0:** • Add an even number of children to the horizon you drew in step 8.
(13) Add clouds. 	**22.29:** • Draw an odd number of clouds in the sky.	**22.3:** • Draw an even number of clouds in the sky.
(14) Decorate the clouds.  	**3.10:** • Shade the clouds you drew in step 13.	**3.010:** • In the clouds you drew in step 13, draw any pattern you wish.
(15) Decorate the top of the tree.  	**0.000010:** • Shade the figure you drew in step 6.	**0.00011:** • In the figure you drew in step 6, draw any pattern you wish.
(16) Decorate the trunk. 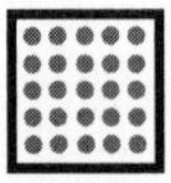 	**3.70:** • In the square you drew in step 5, draw any pattern you wish.	**4.0:** • Shade the square you drew in step 5.

Follow-the-Directions Solve & Draw Math, Grades 6–8 • © 2009 by Merideth Anderson • Scholastic Teaching Resources

Snow-Day Decimals

Materials

* Snow-Day Decimals: Solve It (page 42)
* Snow-Day Decimals: Hidden Picture Directions (pages 43–45)
* Ruler
* Compass
* Copy paper (8 ½ x 14 or larger)
* Pencil

Vocabulary

Arc: a part of a circle

Diameter: a segment passing through the center of a circle with its endpoints on the circle

Horizontal: parallel to the horizon (left to right)

Isosceles triangle: a triangle with exactly two equal sides

Segment: a part of a line with two endpoints

Square: a parallelogram with four right angles and four equal sides

Vertical: perpendicular to the horizon (up and down)

Getting Started

1. Hand out copies of Snow-Day Decimals: Solve It and have students answer the problems.

2. When students have completed the practice page, hand out Snow-Day Decimals: Hidden Picture Directions. Review the steps with students and complete one or two steps with them, reminding them to take their time and read through the steps carefully.

3. To begin the drawing, have students collect the materials listed at left and set their papers vertically (portrait).

4. If students are unfamiliar with using a compass to draw circles and arcs, model the procedure on page 6 before they begin drawing their hidden picture. Steps 1, 2, 3, 6, 7, 9, and 12 require the use of a compass.

5. As you assist students, have them draw the first circle as close to the bottom of the page as possible. Remind them that the figures in steps 10 and 11 can be described as concave dodecagons.

Answers (page 42)

1. 16.2	9. 2
2. 12	10. 68.3
3. 55.27	11. 1.479
4. 0.372	12. 1,400
5. 4.4	13. 2.5
6. 60	14. 300
7. 2,000	15. 0.694
8. 2.19	16. 2.02

Solution to Snow-Day Decimals Hidden Drawing

Name _____ Date _____

Directions: Solve each problem and show your work. Then round your answer.

1 4.09 × 3.96	**2** 4.3 × 2.9	**3** 9.87 × 5.6	**4** .590 × .63
Round to the nearest tenth: _____	Round to the nearest whole number: _____	Round to the nearest hundredth: _____	Round to the nearest thousandth: _____
5 43.59 × 0.1	**6** 5.97 × 10	**7** 43.79 × 42	**8** 0.27 × 8.1
Round to the nearest tenth: _____	Round to the nearest ten: _____	Round to the nearest thousand: _____	Round to the nearest hundredth: _____
9 1.09 × 2.14	**10** 6.7 × 10.2	**11** 0.279 × 5.3	**12** 420 × 3.3
Round to the nearest whole number: _____	Round to the nearest tenth: _____	Round to the nearest thousandth: _____	Round to the nearest hundred: _____
13 2.065 × 1.2	**14** 2.84 × 100	**15** 5.342 × .13	**16** 0.403 × 5
Round to the nearest tenth: _____	Round to the nearest hundred: _____	Round to the nearest thousandth: _____	Round to the nearest hundredth: _____

Follow-the-Directions Solve & Draw Math, Grades 6–8 • © 2009 by Merideth Anderson • Scholastic Teaching Resources

Directions: Use your answers to Snow-Day Decimals: Solve It to choose an answer for each step below. One step at a time, follow the directions to reveal the hidden picture.

Step/Question	If your answer is . . .	
1 Make the body.	**1,619.6:** • Set your compass for a 4-in.-diameter circle. • Draw a circle no more than ½ in. from the bottom of your page.	**16.2:** • Set your compass for a 6-in.-diameter circle. • Draw a circle no more than ½ in. from the bottom of your page.
2 Make the body.	**125:** • Set your compass for a 6-in.-diameter circle. • Draw a circle centered on top of the first circle you drew in step 1.	**12:** • Set your compass for a 5-in.-diameter circle • Draw a circle centered on top of the first circle you drew in step 1.
3 Make the body.	**55.27:** • Set your compass for a 4-in.-diameter circle. • Draw a circle centered on top of the circle you drew in step 2.	**552.27:** • Set your compass for a 6-in.-diameter circle. • Draw a circle centered on top of the circle you drew in step 2.
4 Make the hat.	**0.372:** • Centered on the top of the circle you drew in step 3, draw a 4-in. horizontal line segment.	**3.717:** • Centered on the top of the circle you drew in step 3, draw a 2-in. horizontal line segment.
5 Make the hat.	**4.3:** • Centered on top of the line segment you drew in step 4, draw a 4-in. square.	**4.4:** • Centered on top of the line segment you drew in step 4, draw a 2-in. square.
6 Make an eye.	**59.7:** • Set your compass for a 1½-in.-diameter circle. • On the top right side of the circle you drew in step 3, draw a circle.	**60:** • Set your compass for a 1-in.-diameter circle. • On the top right side of the circle you drew in step 3, draw a circle.
7 Make the other eye.	**2,000:** • Set your compass for a 1-in.-diameter circle. • On the top left side of the circle you drew in step 3, draw a circle.	**1,900:** • Set your compass for a 1½-in.-diameter circle. • On the top left side of the circle you drew in step 3, draw a circle.

Step/Question	If your answer is . . .	
8 Make the nose.	**2.187:** • Draw a scalene triangle with sides measuring 1 in., ½ in., and ¾ in. • Set this triangle below and between the eyes you drew in steps 6 and 7.	**2.19:** • Draw an isosceles triangle with two sides measuring 1 in. and one side measuring ½ in. • Set this triangle below and between the eyes you drew in steps 6 and 7.
9 Make the mouth.	**2:** • Set your compass for a ½-in.-diameter circle. • Draw six circles in an arc below the nose you drew in step 8.	**23:** • Set your compass for a ½-in.-diameter circle. • Draw three circles in an arc below the nose you drew in step 8.
10 Make an arm.	**68.3:** • On the right side of the circle you drew in step 2, draw two parallel line segments extending out. • Connect these segments using nine smaller segments (this should look like a tree branch).	**70:** • On the right side of the circle you drew in step 2, draw two parallel line segments extending out. • Connect these segments using four smaller segments (this should look like a tree branch).
11 Make the other arm.	**14.787:** • On the left side of the circle you drew in step 2, draw two line segments extending out. • Connect these segments using four smaller segments (this should look like a tree branch).	**1.479:** • On the left side of the circle you drew in step 2, draw two line segments extending out. • Connect these segments using nine smaller segments (this should look like a tree branch).
12 Make the buttons.	**1,300:** • Set your compass for a ½-in.-diameter circle. • Centered in the circle you drew in step 2, draw a vertical column of five circles.	**1,400:** • Set your compass for a 1-in.-diameter circle • Centered in the circle you drew in step 2, draw a vertical column of three circles.
13 Decorate the hat.	**2.5:** • In the square you drew in step 5, draw any pattern you wish.	**2.48:** • Shade the square you drew in step 5.

Follow-the-Directions Solve & Draw Math, Grades 6–8 • © 2009 by Merideth Anderson • Scholastic Teaching Resources

Step/Question	If your answer is . . .	
(14) Decorate the eyes.	**200:** • In the circles you drew in steps 6 and 7, draw any pattern you wish.	**300:** • Shade the circles you drew in steps 6 and 7.
(15) Decorate the buttons.	**0.694:** • In the circles you drew in step 12, draw any pattern you wish.	**0.6945:** • Shade the circles you drew in step 12.
(16) Decorate the mouth.	**2.02:** • Shade the circles you drew in step 9.	**0.20:** • In the circles you drew in step 9, draw any pattern you wish.

Dazzling Division

Materials

* Dazzling Division: Solve It (page 47)
* Dazzling Division: Hidden Picture Directions (pages 48–50)
* Ruler
* Compass
* Copy paper (8 ½ x 14 or larger)
* Pencil

Vocabulary

Diameter: a segment passing through the center of a circle with its endpoints on the circle

Equilateral triangle: a triangle with three equal sides

Horizontal: parallel to the horizon (left to right)

Segment: a part of a line with two endpoints

Semicircle: a half of a circle

Getting Started

1. Hand out copies of Dazzling Division: Solve It and have students answer the problems.

2. When students have completed the practice page, hand out the Dazzling Division: Hidden Picture Directions. Review the steps with students and complete one or two steps with them, reminding them to take their time and read through the steps carefully.

3. To begin the drawing, have students collect the materials listed at left and set their papers horizontally (landscape).

4. If students are unfamiliar with using a compass to draw circles and arcs, model the procedure on page 6 before they begin drawing their hidden picture. Steps 4–12 require the use of a compass.

⚡ Fast Finishers

Have students who finish early complete the following story starter: "At the end of the rainbow, I found . . . ." To challenge students, have them include some of the following vocabulary words: *horizontal segment, diameter, semicircle, equilateral triangle, line segment.*

Answers (page 47)

1. 1.55	**9.** 0.73
2. 1.9	**10.** 0.396875
3. 44.3	**11.** 0.05
4. 0.025	**12.** 12.3
5. 0.023	**13.** 41.5
6. 0.375	**14.** 0.25
7. 0.07	**15.** 13.9
8. 0.04	**16.** 38.6

Solution to Dazzling Division Hidden Drawing

Name _____ Date _____

Directions: Solve each problem and show your work.

1 23.25 ÷ 15	**2** 155.8 ÷ 82	**3** 664.5 ÷ 15	**4** 0.4 ÷ 16
5 2.3 ÷ 100	**6** 3 ÷ 8	**7** 7 ÷ 100	**8** 0.4 ÷ 10
9 6.497 ÷ 8.9	**10** 2.54 ÷ 6.4	**11** 0.04 ÷ 0.8	**12** 75.03 ÷ 6.1
13 $0.3x = 12.45$	**14** $6.64t = 1.66$	**15** $0.05r = 0.695$	**16** $1.7x = 65.62$

Directions: Use your answers to Dazzling Division: Solve It to choose an answer for each step below. One step at a time, follow the directions to reveal the hidden picture.

Step/Question	If your answer is . . .	
(1) Make the base. ————————	**1.55:** • Measure up 2 in. from the bottom of the page and draw a 12-in. horizontal segment. • Center the line between the sides of the page.	**1.1667:** • Measure up 2 in. from the bottom of the page and draw a 6-in. horizontal segment. • Center the line between the sides of the page.
(2) Make the base.	**0.19:** • From the left endpoint on the segment you drew in step 1, measure 2 in. to the right and make a mark. • Continue marking the line every 2 in. toward the center of the page, making a total of seven marks.	**1.9:** • From the left endpoint on the segment you drew in step 1, measure ¾ in. to the right and make a mark. • Continue marking the line every ¾ in. toward the center of the page, making a total of seven marks.
(3) Make the base.	**44.03:** • From the right endpoint on the segment you drew in step 1, measure 2 in. to the left and make a mark. • Continue marking the line every 2 in. toward the center of the page, making a total of seven marks.	**44.3:** • From the right endpoint on the segment you drew in step 1, measure ¾ in. to the left and make a mark. • Continue marking the line every ¾ in. toward the center of the page, making a total of seven marks.
(4) Make the rainbow.	**0.4:** • Set your compass for a 10-in.-diameter circle. • Place the pencil tip on one end of the segment you drew in step 1. • Draw a semicircle above the segment that connects to the other end of the segment.	**0.025:** • Set your compass for a 12-in.-diameter circle. • Place the pencil tip on one end of the segment you drew in step 1. • Draw a semicircle above the segment that connects to the other end of the segment.
(5) Make the rainbow.	**0.023:** • Set your compass for a 10½-in.-diameter circle. • Place the pencil tip on the first mark you made in step 2. • Draw a semicircle above the segment that connects to the first mark you made in step 3.	**0.23:** • Set your compass for an 8-in.-diameter circle. • Place the pencil tip on the first mark you made in step 2. • Draw a semicircle above the segment that connects to the first mark you made in step 3.

Follow-the-Directions Solve & Draw Math, Grades 6–8 • © 2009 by Merideth Anderson • Scholastic Teaching Resources

Step/Question	If your answer is . . .	
6 Make the rainbow.	**2.667:** • Set your compass for an 8-in.-diameter circle. • Place the pencil tip on the second mark you made in step 2. • Draw a semicircle above the segment that connects to the second mark you made in step 3.	**0.375:** • Set your compass for a 9-in.-diameter circle. • Place the pencil tip on the second mark you made in step 2. • Draw a semicircle above the segment that connects to the second mark you made in step 3.
7 Make the rainbow.	**0.07:** • Set your compass for a 7½-in.-diameter circle. • Place the pencil tip on the third mark you made in step 2. • Draw a semicircle above the segment that connects to the third mark you made in step 3.	**0.7:** • Set your compass for a 6-in.-diameter circle. • Place the pencil tip on the third mark you made in step 2. • Draw a semicircle above the segment that connects to the third mark you made in step 3.
8 Make the rainbow.	**0.4:** • Set your compass for a 5-in.-diameter circle. • Place the pencil tip on the fourth mark you made in step 2. • Draw a semicircle above the segment that connects to the fourth mark you made in step 3.	**0.04:** • Set your compass for a 6-in.-diameter circle. • Place the pencil tip on the fourth mark you made in step 2. • Draw a semicircle above the segment that connects to the fourth mark you made in step 3.
9 Make the rainbow.	**0.073:** • Set your compass for a 3-in.-diameter circle. • Place the pencil tip on the fifth mark you made in step 2. • Draw a semicircle above the segment that connects to the fifth mark you made in step 3.	**0.73:** • Set your compass for a 4½-in.-diameter circle. • Place the pencil tip on the fifth mark you made in step 2. • Draw a semicircle above the segment that connects to the fifth mark you made in step 3.
10 Make the rainbow.	**0.30906080705:** • Set your compass for a 2-in.-diameter circle. • Place the pencil tip on the sixth mark you made in step 2. • Draw a semicircle above the segment that connects to the sixth mark you made in step 3.	**0.396875:** • Set your compass for a 3-in.-diameter circle. • Place the pencil tip on the sixth mark you made in step 2. • Draw a semicircle above the segment that connects to the sixth mark you made in step 3.

Step/Question	If your answer is . . .	
11 Make the rainbow. 11 1 2 3	**0.05:** • Set your compass for a 1½-in.-diameter circle. • Place the pencil tip on the seventh mark you made in step 2. • Draw a semicircle above the segment connecting to the seventh mark you made in step 3.	**0.2:** • Set your compass for a ½-in.-diameter circle. • Place the pencil tip on the seventh mark you made in step 2. • Draw a semicircle above the segment that connects to the seventh mark you made in step 3.
12 Make the sun.	**102.3:** • Set your compass for a 3-in.-diameter circle • Draw a circle in the upper right corner of the page.	**12.3:** • Set your compass for a 3-in.-diameter circle. • Draw a circle in the upper left corner of the page.
13 Make the sun rays. 12 13	**3.735:** • Draw an odd number of 1-in. rays extending from the sun you drew in step 12.	**41.5:** • Draw an even number of 1-in. rays extending from the sun you drew in step 12.
14 Make clouds.	**0.25:** • Draw an odd number of clouds in the sky.	**11.0224:** • Draw an even number of clouds in the sky.
15 Make raindrops.	**0.03475:** • Draw raindrops falling from fewer than half of the clouds.	**13.9:** • Draw raindrops falling from at least half of the clouds.
16 Final touches. or	**111.554:** • In the clouds, draw any pattern you wish.	**38.6:** • Shade the clouds.

Follow-the-Directions Solve & Draw Math, Grades 6–8 • © 2009 by Merideth Anderson • Scholastic Teaching Resources

Icky Integers

Materials

* Icky Integers: Solve It (page 52)
* Icky Integers: Hidden Picture Directions (pages 53–55)
* Ruler
* Compass
* Copy paper (8½ x 14 or larger)
* Pencil
* Protractor

Vocabulary

Diameter: a segment passing through the center of a circle with its endpoints on the circle

Horizontal: parallel to the horizon (left to right)

Oblique segment: a segment that is neither vertical nor horizontal

Palindrome: a word that is spelled the same forward as it is backward

Perpendicular: segments that intersect to form right angles

Rectangle: a parallelogram with four right angles

Vertical: perpendicular to the horizon (up and down)

Getting Started

1. Hand out copies of Icky Integers: Solve It and have students answer the problems.

2. When students have completed the practice page, hand out Icky Integers: Hidden Picture Directions. Review the steps with students and complete one or two steps with them, reminding them to take their time and read through the steps carefully.

3. To begin the drawing, have students collect the materials listed at left and set their papers vertically (portrait).

4. If students are unfamiliar with using a compass to draw circles and arcs, model the procedure on page 6 before students begin drawing their hidden picture. Step 12 requires the use of a compass.

5. If students are unfamiliar with using a protractor to draw angles, model the procedure on page 6 before they begin drawing their hidden picture. Steps 3, 4, and 6 require the use of a protractor.

6. As you assist students, remind them that the rectangle (step 1) needs to be 3 in. from the top of the page or they will run out of room. If necessary, give them examples of palindromes—*Bob, Hannah, Mom, Dad,* and so on.

Answers (page 52)

1. 36	**9.** 56
2. 18	**10.** -105
3. -5	**11.** -180
4. -141	**12.** -3
5. 53	**13.** -29
6. -16	**14.** 233
7. -27	**15.** -37
8. -1	**16.** -38

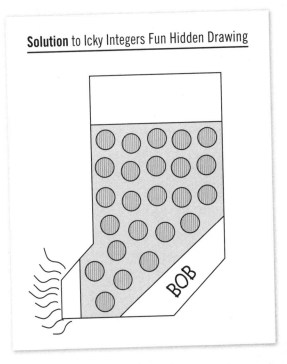

Solution to Icky Integers Fun Hidden Drawing

Name _____ Date _____

Directions: Evaluate each expression and show your work.

1 $(-4)^2 + 10 \times 2$	**2** $9 + (7 - 4)^2$	**3** $2^3 + (8 - 5) \times 4 - 5^2$	**4** $2^3 \times 3 - 5(5^2 + 8)$
5 $5 \times 3^2 + 8$	**6** $-6^2 + 3^3 - 7$	**7** $-62 - (-59) - 24$	**8** $-4 + 12 + (-3) + (-6)$
9 $(-6)^2 + 3^3 - 7$	**10** $2^2 \times 3 - 5 \times 5^2 + 8$	**11** $5(-12)(-3)(-1)$	**12** $250 \div (-50) + 5 + (-3)$
13 $(2^3 + 8) - 5 \times 4 - 5^2$	**14** $(5 \times 3)^2 + 8$	**15** $-120 \div 40 + 17 \times (-2)$	**16** $4 + 7 \times 2 + 8(-7)$

Follow-the-Directions Solve & Draw Math, Grades 6–8 • © 2009 by Merideth Anderson • Scholastic Teaching Resources

Directions: Use your answers to Icky Integers: Solve It to choose an answer for each step below. One step at a time, follow the directions to reveal the hidden picture.

Step/Question	If your answer is . . .	
1 Make the cuff.	**-12:** • Measuring down 3 in. from the top of your paper, draw a rectangle with a base of 3½ in. and a height of 1¼ in. • Center the rectangle between the sides of your page.	**36:** • Measuring down 3 in. from the top of your paper, draw a rectangle with a base of 7 in. and a height of 2½ in. • Center the rectangle between the sides of your page.
2 Make the sock.	**18:** • From the bottom right corner of the rectangle you drew in step 1, draw a 7-in. vertical segment extending down.	**0:** • From the bottom right corner of the rectangle you drew in step 1, draw a 3-in. vertical segment extending down.
3 Make the sock.	**-5:** • Use the segment you drew in step 2 as the base and the bottom endpoint as the vertex to make a 134° angle. • Draw a 4-in. oblique line segment extending down and left.	**8:** • Use the segment you drew in step 2 as the base and the bottom endpoint as the vertex to make a 120° angle. • Draw a 1-in. oblique line segment extending down and left.
4 Make the sock.	**-72:** • Use the segment you drew in step 3 as the base and the bottom endpoint as the vertex to make a 135° angle. • Draw a 1-in. oblique segment extending left.	**-141:** • Use the segment you drew in step 3 as the base and the bottom endpoint as the vertex to make a 140° angle. • Draw a 6-in. oblique segment extending left.
5 Make the sock.	**38:** • From the left endpoint of the segment you drew in step 4, draw a 4-in. vertical segment extending up.	**53:** • From the left endpoint of the segment you drew in step 4, draw a 2-in. vertical segment extending up.
6 Make the sock.	**-16:** • Use the segment you drew in step 5 as the base and the left endpoint as the vertex to make a 125° angle. • Draw a 2½-in. oblique segment extending up and right.	**-70:** • Use the segment you drew in step 5 as the base and the left endpoint as the vertex to make a 145° angle. • Draw a 5-in. oblique segment extending up and right.

Step/Question	If your answer is . . .	
(7) Make the toe.	**-145:** • From the bottom endpoint of the segment you drew in step 6, measure up 1 in. and make a mark.	**-27:** • From the bottom endpoint of the segment you drew in step 6, measure up 2 in. and make a mark.
(8) Make the toe	**-1:** • From the left endpoint of the segment you drew in step 4, measure 1 in. to the right and make a mark. • Connect this mark to the mark you made in step 7.	**-25:** • From the left endpoint of the segment you drew in step 4, measure 2 in. to the right and make a mark. • Connect this mark to the mark you made in step 7.
(9) Make the sock.	**56:** • From the top endpoint of the segment you drew in step 6, draw a 6¼-in. vertical segment extending up. • Make sure this segment meets the bottom left corner of the rectangle you drew in step 1.	**32:** • From the top endpoint of the segment you drew in step 6, draw a 5-in. vertical segment extending up. • Make sure this segment meets the bottom left corner of the rectangle you drew in step 1.
(10) Make the heel.	**8:** • From the bottom endpoint of the segment you drew in step 2, measure up ¼ in. and make a mark.	**-105:** • From the bottom endpoint of the segment you drew in step 2, measure up 1¼ in. and make a mark.
(11) Make the heel.	**180:** • From the right endpoint of the segment you drew in step 4, measure 3 in. to the left, and make a mark. • Connect this mark with the one you made in step 10.	**-180:** • From the right endpoint of the segment you drew in step 4, measure 1½ in. to the left, and make a mark. • Connect this mark with the one you made in step 10.
(12) Decorate the sock.	**-3:** • Set your compass for a 1-in.-diameter circle. • Draw 24 circles on your sock.	**7:** • Set your compass for a 2-in.-diameter circle. • Draw 20 circles on your sock.
(13) Decorate the heel.	**-31:** • Write your name on the heel of the sock.	**-29:** • On the heel of the sock, write a palindrome that is also a person's name.

Follow-the-Directions Solve & Draw Math, Grades 6–8 • © 2009 by Merideth Anderson • Scholastic Teaching Resources

Step/Question	If your answer is . . .	
(14) Decorate the sock.	**233:** • Draw an odd number of squiggly lines extending out from the toe of the sock to show that it's smelly.	**38:** • Draw an even number of squiggly lines extending out from the toe of the sock to show that it's smelly.
(15) Decorate the sock. ○ or ○	**37:** • In the circles you drew in step 12, draw horizontal stripes.	**-37:** • In the circles you drew in step 12, draw vertical stripes.
(16) Decorate the sock. or	**-38:** • Shade the area of your sock between the cuff and toe that is not covered by circles.	**74:** • In the area of your sock between the cuff and toe that is not covered by circles, draw any pattern you wish.

Expressions Are Doggone Fun

Materials

* Expressions Are Doggone Fun: Solve It (page 57)
* Expressions Are Doggone Fun: Hidden Picture Directions (pages 58–60)
* Ruler
* Compass
* Protractor
* Copy paper (8 ½ x 14 or larger)
* Pencil

Vocabulary

Diameter: a segment passing through the center of a circle with its endpoints on the circle

Horizontal: parallel to the horizon (left to right)

Oblique segment: a segment that is neither vertical nor horizontal

Quadrilateral: a four-sided polygon

Segment: a part of a line with two endpoints

Vertical: perpendicular to the horizon (up and down)

Getting Started

1. Hand out copies of Expressions are Doggone Fun: Solve It and have students answer the problems.

2. When students have completed the practice page, hand out the Expressions are Doggone Fun: Hidden Picture Directions pages. Review the steps with students and complete one or two steps with them, reminding them to take their time and read through the steps carefully.

3. To begin the drawing, have students collect the materials listed at left and set their papers horizontally (landscape).

4. If students are unfamiliar with using a compass to draw circles and arcs, model the procedure on page 6 before they begin drawing their hidden picture. Step 16 requires the use of a compass.

5. If students are unfamiliar with using a protractor to draw angles, model the procedure on page 6 before students begin drawing their hidden picture. Steps 3–7, 14, and 15 require the use of a protractor.

6. As you assist students, allow them to design the nose, eye, mouth, and collar in their own way as long as the nose is a square and the eye is a circle.

⚡ Fast Finishers

Have students who finish early give their dog a name, and draw a background. Then have students write a day's schedule for a doggie day camp. Encourage them to include games and activities dogs would enjoy, nap time, and meal time. Challenge students by having them use some of the following vocabulary words in their writing: *oblique segment, horizontal, vertical, quadrilateral, diameter.*

Answers (page 57)

1. 23	**9.** 5
2. 2	**10.** 54
3. 48	**11.** 40
4. 15	**12.** 7½
5. 2	**13.** 1
6. 52	**14.** 38
7. 144	**15.** 5
8. 12	**16.** ⅔

Solution to Expressions Are Doggone Fun

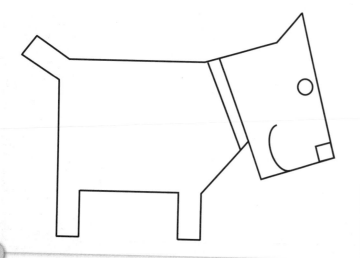

Name _____ Date _____

Directions: Solve each expression for **a = 4**, **b = 6**, and **c = 2** and show your work.

1 $5a + 3$	**2** $3b - 4a$	**3** abc	**4** $\dfrac{b}{c} + 3a$
5 $(b + c) \div a$	**6** $a^2 + b^2$	**7** $(a + b + c)^2$	**8** $13 - 0.5c$
9 $\dfrac{(2.5\,c + 5)}{c}$	**10** $30 + 2bc$	**11** $4(a + b)$	**12** $ab \div 3.2$
13 $\dfrac{abc}{abc}$	**14** $\sqrt{a} + b^2$	**15** $\sqrt{ab + c - 1}$	**16** $|-a| \div |-b|$

Expressions Are Doggone Fun: Hidden Picture Directions

Directions: Use your answers to Expressions Are Doggone Fun: Solve It to choose an answer for each step below. One step at a time, follow the directions to reveal the hidden picture.

Step/Question	If your answer is . . .	
1 Make the body. _____	**23:** • Measure down 4 in. from the top of the page. • Draw a 5-in. horizontal segment, centered between the sides of the page.	**57:** • Measure down 4 in. from the top of the page. • Draw a 8-in. horizontal segment, centered between the sides of the page.
2 Make the head.	**-6:** • Use the segment you drew in step 1 as the base and the right endpoint as the vertex to make a 20° angle. • Draw a 2-in. segment extending up and right.	**2:** • Use the segment you drew in step 1 as the base and the right endpoint as the vertex to make a 160° angle. • Draw a 2½-in. segment extending up and right.
3 Make the ear.	**48:** • Use the segment you drew in step 2 as the base and the right endpoint as the vertex to make a 130° angle. • Draw a 1¼-in. segment extending up and right.	**462:** • Use the segment you drew in step 2 as the base and the right endpoint as the vertex to make a 130° angle. • Draw a 3-in. segment extending up and right.
4 Make the head.	**37:** • Use the segment you drew in step 3 as the base and the top endpoint as the vertex to make a 40° angle. • Draw a 4-in. segment extending down.	**15:** • Use the segment you drew in step 3 as the base and the top endpoint as the vertex to make a 40° angle. • Draw a 4¾-in. segment extending down.
5 Make the head.	**2:** • Use the segment you drew in step 4 as the base and the bottom endpoint as the vertex to make a 95° angle. • Draw a 2½-in. segment extending left.	**3:** • Use the segment you drew in step 4 as the base and the bottom endpoint as the vertex to make a 95° angle. • Draw a 3-in. segment extending left.

58

Step/Question	If your answer is . . .	
6 Make the head.	**20:** • Use the segment you drew in step 5 as the base and the left endpoint as the vertex to make a right angle. • Draw a 3-in. line segment extending up.	**52:** • Use the segment you drew in step 5 as the base and the left endpoint as the vertex to make a right angle. • Draw a 4-in. line segment extending up.
7 Make the body.	**24:** • From the bottom endpoint of the segment you drew in step 6, measure up 2 in. and make a mark on the line. • Use this point as the vertex to make a 75° angle, drawing a 3-in. line segment extending down and left.	**144:** • From the bottom endpoint of the segment you drew in step 6, measure up 1¼ in. and make a mark on the line. • Use this point as the vertex to make a 75° angle, drawing a 2-in. line segment extending down and left.
8 Make a leg.	**12:** • From the bottom endpoint of the segment you drew in step 7, draw a 1½-in. vertical line segment extending down.	**25:** • From the bottom endpoint of the segment you drew in step 7, draw a 1-in. vertical line segment extending down.
9 Make a leg.	**7.5:** • From the bottom endpoint of the segment you drew in step 8, draw a ¼-in. horizontal segment extending left.	**5:** • From the bottom endpoint of the segment you drew in step 8, draw a ¾-in. horizontal segment extending left.
10 Make a leg.	**54:** • From the left endpoint of the segment you drew in step 9, draw a 1½-in. vertical segment extending up.	**384:** • From the left endpoint of the segment you drew in step 9, draw a ½-in. vertical segment extending up.
11 Make the body.	**22:** • From the top endpoint of the segment you drew in step 10, draw a 2¾-in. horizontal segment extending left.	**40:** • From the top endpoint of the segment you drew in step 10, draw a 3¼-in. horizontal segment extending left.

Step/Question	If your answer is . . .	
12 Make the other leg.	**7.5:** • From the left endpoint of the segment you drew in step 11, draw a vertical segment extending 1 ½ in. down. • From the bottom endpoint of the segment you just drew, draw a horizontal line extending ¾ in. to the left.	**7.05:** • From the left endpoint of the segment you drew in step 11, draw a vertical segment extending 3 in. down. • From the bottom endpoint of the segment you just drew, draw a horizontal line extending 1 in. to the left.
13 Make the body.	**0:** • From the left endpoint of the horizontal segment you drew in step 12, draw a 6-in. vertical segment extending up.	**1:** • From the left endpoint of the horizontal segment you drew in step 12, draw a 5-in. vertical segment extending up.
14 Make the tail.	**38:** • Use the segment you drew in step 13 as the base and the top endpoint as the vertex of a 130° angle. • Draw a 1½-in. segment extending up and left.	**14:** • Use the segment you drew in step 13 as the base and the top endpoint as the vertex of a 130° angle. • Draw a 2-in. segment extending up and left.
15 Finish the tail.	**5.3:** • Use the segment you drew in step 14 as the base and the top endpoint as the vertex to make a right angle. • Draw a 1½-in. segment extending up and right. • Connect the end of this segment to the left endpoint of the segment you drew in step 1.	**5:** • Use the segment you drew in step 14 as the base and the top endpoint as the vertex to make a right angle. • Draw a ¾-in. segment extending up and right. • Connect the end of this segment to the left endpoint of the segment you drew in step 1.
16 Add finishing touches.	**-0.67:** • Draw a circle nose, about ½ in. in diameter. • Draw a square eye with ½-in. sides. • Toward the bottom of the segment you drew in step 5, draw a mouth. • Draw a collar.	**0.67:** • Draw a square nose with ½ in. sides. • Draw a circle eye with a ½-in. diameter. • Toward the bottom of the segment you drew in step 5, draw a mouth. • Draw a collar.

Follow-the-Directions Solve & Draw Math, Grades 6–8 • © 2009 by Merideth Anderson • Scholastic Teaching Resources

Fancy Over Fractions

Materials

* Fancy Over Fractions: Solve It (page 62)
* Fancy Over Fractions: Hidden Picture Directions (pages 63–65)
* Ruler
* Compass
* Copy paper (8½ x 14 or larger)
* Pencil
* Protractor

Vocabulary

Arc: a part of a circle

Diameter: a segment passing through the center of a circle with its endpoints on the circle

Equilateral triangle: a triangle with three equal sides

Horizontal: parallel to the horizon (left to right)

Oblique segment: a segment that is neither vertical nor horizontal

Parallelogram: a quadrilateral with two pairs of parallel sides

Perpendicular: segments that intersect to form right angles

Rectangle: a parallelogram with four right angles

Trapezoid: a quadrilateral with exactly one pair of parallel sides

Vertical: perpendicular to the horizon (up and down)

Getting Started

1. Hand out copies of Fancy Over Fractions: Solve It and have students answer the problems.

2. When students have completed the practice page, hand out Fancy Over Fractions: Hidden Picture Directions. Review the steps with students and complete one or two steps with them, reminding them to take their time and read through the steps carefully.

3. To begin the drawing, have students collect the materials listed at left and set their papers vertically (portrait).

4. If students are unfamiliar with using a compass to draw circles and arcs, model the procedure on page 6 before they begin drawing their hidden picture. Steps 1, 13, 14, and 15 require the use of a compass.

5. If students are unfamiliar with using a protractor to draw angles, model the procedure on page 6 before students begin drawing their hidden picture. Step 8 requires the use of a protractor.

6. As you assist students, remind them that their drawing needs to be centered horizontally so it will fit.

Solution to Fancy Over Fractions Hidden Drawing

Answers (page 62)

1. $1\frac{5}{8}$	**9.** $\frac{8}{9}$
2. $1\frac{1}{24}$	**10.** $6\frac{1}{4}$
3. $9\frac{1}{8}$	**11.** $2\frac{1}{8}$
4. $3\frac{5}{8}$	**12.** $5\frac{2}{5}$
5. $2\frac{19}{40}$	**13.** $2\frac{3}{8}$
6. $5\frac{1}{4}$	**14.** $6\frac{1}{2}$
7. 0	**15.** $\frac{5}{12}$
8. $7\frac{1}{3}$	**16.** $\frac{1}{8}$

Fancy Over Fractions: Solve It

Name _____ Date _____

Directions: Solve each problem, show your work, and reduce the answer.

1 $j - \dfrac{3}{4} = \dfrac{7}{8}$	**2** $\dfrac{1}{6} = g - \dfrac{7}{8}$	**3** $\dfrac{5}{8} + t = 9\dfrac{3}{4}$	**4** $6\dfrac{1}{2} = m + 2\dfrac{7}{8}$
5 $\dfrac{2}{5} + m = 2\dfrac{7}{8}$	**6** $w - 3\dfrac{1}{2} = 1\dfrac{3}{4}$	**7** $x + \dfrac{1}{2} = \dfrac{11}{22}$	**8** $10 = y + 2\dfrac{2}{3}$
9 $\dfrac{2}{3} = p - \dfrac{2}{9}$	**10** $z - 1\dfrac{3}{4} = 4\dfrac{1}{2}$	**11** $a - \dfrac{7}{8} = 1\dfrac{1}{4}$	**12** $p + \dfrac{4}{5} = 6\dfrac{1}{5}$
13 $q - \dfrac{1}{4} = 2\dfrac{1}{8}$	**14** $t - 2\dfrac{1}{5} = 4\dfrac{3}{10}$	**15** $x + \dfrac{1}{2} = \dfrac{11}{12}$	**16** $\dfrac{1}{2} + y = \dfrac{5}{8}$

Follow-the-Directions Solve & Draw Math, Grades 6–8 • © 2009 by Merideth Anderson • Scholastic Teaching Resources

Fancy Over Fractions: Hidden Picture Directions

Directions: Use your answers to Fancy Over Fractions: Solve It to choose an answer for each step below. One step at a time, follow the directions to reveal the hidden picture.

Step/Question	If your answer is . . .	
1 Make the head. 	**$\frac{1}{8}$:** • Set your compass for a 6-in.-diameter circle. • Measure down $4\frac{1}{2}$ in. from the top center of the page. • Draw a circle (the top of the circle will touch the $4\frac{1}{2}$-in. mark).	**$1\frac{5}{8}$:** • Set your compass for a 4-in.-diameter circle. • Measure down $4\frac{1}{2}$ in. from the top center of the page. • Draw a circle (the top of the circle will touch the $4\frac{1}{2}$-in. mark).
2 Make the body. 	**$1\frac{1}{24}$:** • Place your pencil on the bottom of the circle you drew in step 1. • Draw a trapezoid centered on this point with a 3-in. top, 6-in. sides, and a $7\frac{1}{8}$-in. bottom. • Draw a large heart in the center of the trapezoid.	**$1\frac{7}{24}$:** • Place your pencil on the bottom of the circle you drew in step 1. • Draw a trapezoid centered on this point with a 2-in. top, 9-in. sides, and an 11-in. bottom. • Draw a large heart in the center of the trapezoid.
3 Make the legs. 	**$10\frac{3}{8}$:** • From the bottom left corner of the trapezoid, measure 2 in. to the right. • Draw a 2-in. vertical segment extending down. • Repeat this step from the bottom right corner of the trapezoid, measuring to the left.	**$9\frac{1}{8}$:** • From the bottom left corner of the trapezoid, measure over $1\frac{1}{2}$ in. to the right. • Draw a $2\frac{3}{8}$-in. vertical segment extending down. • Repeat this step from the bottom right corner of the trapezoid, measuring to the left.
4 Make the legs. 	**$9\frac{3}{8}$:** • From the top of each segment you drew in step 3, measure $\frac{1}{2}$ in. toward the center of the page, and make a mark. • Draw a 2-in. vertical line segment extending down from each mark.	**$3\frac{5}{8}$:** • From the top of each segment you drew in step 3, measure 1 in. toward the center of the page, and make a mark. • Draw a 3-in. vertical line segment extending down from each mark.
5 Make the feet. 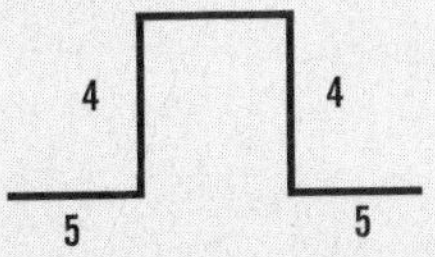	**$2\frac{19}{40}$:** • From the bottom of one of the segments you drew in step 4, draw a 2-in. horizontal segment extending toward the outside of the page. • Repeat this step with the other segment you drew in step 4.	**$3\frac{11}{40}$:** • From the bottom of one of the segments you drew in step 4, draw a 3-in. horizontal segment extending toward the outside of the page. • Repeat this step with the other segment you drew in step 4.

Step/Question	If your answer is . . .	
6 Complete the feet. 6 5 [left] 5 6 [right]	**2¼:** • From each of the outer endpoints of the segments you drew in step 5, draw a 1-in. vertical segment extending up. • Repeat this step on the other segment you drew in step 5.	**5¼:** • From each of the outer endpoints of the segments you drew in step 5, draw a ⅝-in. vertical segment extending up. • Repeat this step on the other segment you drew in step 5.
7 Finish the legs. 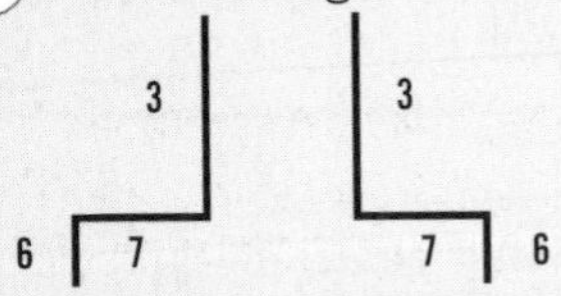3 3 6 7 7 6	**0:** • For both legs, draw a 1¼-in. horizontal segment connecting the segments you drew in steps 6 and 3.	**1:** • For both legs, draw a 2-in. horizontal segment connecting the segments you drew in steps 6 and 3.
8 Make the arms. 8 8 2	**12⅗:** • From the bottom right corner of the trapezoid you drew in step 2, measure up the right edge 2 in. • Use this point as the vertex to make a 99° angle, drawing a 1-in. segment extending up and out. • Repeat this step on the opposite side of the trapezoid.	**7⅓:** • From the bottom right corner of the trapezoid you drew in step 2, measure up the right edge 3 in. • Use this point as the vertex to make a 99° angle, drawing a 2¼-in. segment extending up and out. • Repeat this step on the opposite side of the trapezoid.
9 Make the arms. 9 9 8 8 2	**⅖:** • From the bottom of the segment you drew in step 8, measure up the right edge ½ in. • Draw a 3-in. oblique segment parallel to the segment you drew in step 8. • Repeat this step on the opposite side of the trapezoid.	**8/9:** • From the bottom of the segment you drew in step 8, measure up the right edge 1 in. • Draw a 2-in. oblique segment parallel to the segment you drew in step 8. • Repeat this step on the opposite side of the trapezoid.
10 Make the arms. 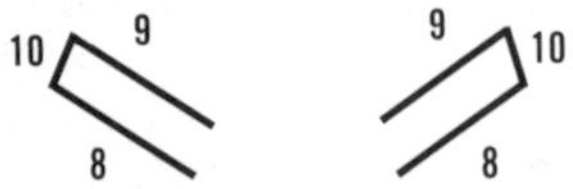10 9 8 9 10 8	**6¼:** • Connect the segments you drew in steps 8 and 9 with a 1-in. segment.	**5⅗:** • Connect the segments you drew in steps 8 and 9 with a 1½-in. segment.
11 Make the arrow. 11 11 11 10 11 11	**⅜:** • On the right side, extend the segment you drew in step 10 by 1 in. in both directions. • Using this segment as the left side of the arrow shaft, draw a rectangle measuring 1 in. wide by 4 in. high.	**2⅛:** • On the right side, extend the segment you drew in step 10 by 1 in. in both directions. • Using this segment as the left side of the arrow shaft, draw a rectangle measuring ½ in. wide by 3 in. high.

Follow-the-Directions Solve & Draw Math, Grades 6–8 • © 2009 by Merideth Anderson • Scholastic Teaching Resources

Step/Question	If your answer is . . .	
12 Make the arrowhead and feathers.  	**5⅖:** • At the top of the rectangle you drew in step 11, draw a ½-in. equilateral triangle. • On the opposite end of the rectangle, draw four parallelograms (two extending out from each side of the rectangle).	**7:** • At the top end of the rectangle you drew in step 11, draw a 2-in. equilateral triangle. • On the opposite end, draw six parallelograms (three extending out from each side of the rectangle).
13 Make the bow. 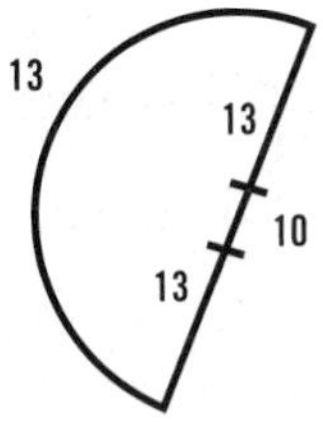	**2⅜:** • Extending from each endpoint of the segment you drew in step 10 (left arm), draw a 2-in. oblique segment. • Connect the endpoints with an arc.	**1⅞:** • Extending from each endpoint of the segment you drew in step 10 (left arm), draw a 3-in. oblique segment. • Connect the endpoints with an arc.
14 Make the eyes.  	**6⅖:** • Draw two 1-in. squares side by side near the top of the circle you drew in step 1. • Draw a heart in the center of each of the squares.	**6½:** • Set your compass for a 1-in.-diameter circle. • Draw two circles side by side near the top of the circle you drew in step 1. • Draw a heart in the center of each of the circles.
15 Make the nose. 	**1:** • Set your compass for a 1-in.-diameter circle. • Draw a circle below and between the eyes you drew in step 14.	**5/12:** • Set your compass for a ½-in.-diameter circle. • Draw a circle below and between the eyes you drew in step 14.
16 Make the mouth. 	**⅛:** • From the bottom of the circle you drew in step 15, measure down ½ in. and draw a 2½-in. horizontal segment. • On each endpoint of this segment, draw a ½-in. vertical segment extending up.	**1⅛:** • From the bottom of the circle you drew in step 15, measure down ½ in. and draw a 1-in. horizontal segment.

Follow-the-Directions Solve & Draw Math, Grades 6–8 • © 2009 by Merideth Anderson • Scholastic Teaching Resources

Luck o' the Integer

Materials

* Luck o' the Integer: Solve It (page 67)
* Luck o' the Integer: Hidden Picture Directions (pages 68–70)
* Ruler
* Compass
* Protractor
* Copy paper (8 ½ x 14 or larger)
* Pencil

Vocabulary

Acute angle: an angle less than 90º

Equilateral triangle: a triangle with three equal sides

Horizontal: parallel to the horizon (left to right)

Oblique segment: a segment that is neither vertical nor horizontal

Parallel segments: segments that lie in the same plane but never intersect

Segment: a part of a line with two endpoints

Square: a parallelogram with four right angles and four equal sides

Trapezoid: a quadrilateral with exactly one pair of parallel sides

Vertical: perpendicular to the horizon (up and down)

Getting Started

1. Hand out copies of Luck o' the Integer: Solve It and have students answer the problems.

2. When students have completed the practice page, hand out Luck o' the Integer: Hidden Picture Directions. Review the steps with students and complete one or two steps with them, reminding them to take their time and read through the steps carefully.

3. To begin the drawing, have students collect the materials listed at left and set their papers vertically (portrait).

4. If students are unfamiliar with using a compass to draw circles and arcs, model the procedure on page 6 before they begin drawing their hidden picture. Step 3 requires the use of a compass.

5. If students are unfamiliar with using a protractor to draw angles, model the procedure on page 6 before students begin drawing their hidden picture. Steps 1, 8, 9, 11, 13, 14, and 15 require the use of a protractor.

6. As you assist students, remind them of the following: the hexagon in step 1 must be centered horizontally and exactly 3 in. from the top of the page; step 3 will form a four-leaf clover; and all segments crossing the clover and the buckle can be erased to help clean up the picture.

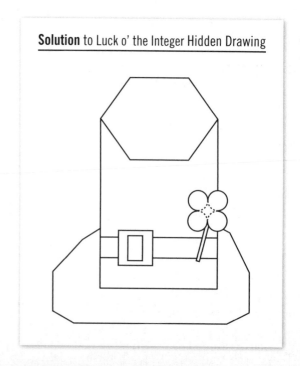

Solution to Luck o' the Integer Hidden Drawing

Answers (page 67)	**6.** -163	**12.** -4,896
1. 38	**7.** -3,607	**13.** -7
2. -4	**8.** 52	**14.** -53
3. -2	**9.** -840	**15.** 2
4. 34	**10.** -612	**16.** 25
5. -114	**11.** 45	

Name _____ Date _____

Directions: Solve each problem and show your work.

1 -99 + 137	**2** 28 + (-32)	**3** -50 + 48	**4** 126 + (-92)
5 124 – 238	**6** -53 + (-110)	**7** -1,302 – 2,305	**8** -52 – (-104)
9 -35(24)	**10** 102(-6)	**11** -15(-3)	**12** -72 × 68
13 84 ÷ (-12)	**14** -106 ÷ 2	**15** -98 ÷ (-49)	**16** (-125) ÷ (-5)

Directions: Use your answers to Luck o' the Integer: Solve It to choose an answer for each step below. One step at a time, follow the directions to reveal the hidden picture.

Step/Question	If your answer is . . .	
(1) Draw the top of the hat.	**-236:** • In the top center of the page draw a convex hexagon with the following measurements: 4 in. (top and bottom) and 3 in. (sides). • Connect the sides, the top, and bottom with 110° angles.	**38:** • In the top center of the page draw a convex hexagon with the following measurements: 3 in. (top and bottom) and 2 in. (sides). • Connect the sides, the top, and bottom with 130° angles.
(2) Draw the sides of the hat.	**60:** • From the vertices of each acute angle you drew in step 1, draw a 10-in. vertical segment extending down.	**-4:** • From the vertices of each acute angle you drew in step 1, draw an 8½-in. vertical segment extending down.
(3) Make a four-leaf clover.	**-2:** • Measure down 3¾ in. from the top endpoint of the right-hand segment you drew in step 2. • Set your compass for a 1-in.-diameter circle. • Draw four circles in the shape of a square. • Erase all the lines inside the square formed by the circles. • Draw a thin rectangular stem, about 2 in. long.	**2:** • Measure down 3¾ in. from the top endpoint of the right-hand segment you drew in step 2. • Draw four 1-in. equilateral triangles radiating from a center point. • Draw a thin rectangular stem, about 2 in. long.
(4) Make the base of the hat.	**34:** • Place your pencil on the bottom endpoint of the right-hand segment you drew in step 2. • Draw a 5½-in. horizontal segment connecting to the bottom endpoint of the left-hand segment you drew in step 2.	**-34:** • Place your pencil on the bottom endpoint of the right-hand segment you drew in step 2. • Draw a 6-in. horizontal segment connecting to the bottom endpoint of the left-hand segment you drew in step 2.
(5) Make the band.	**-114:** • Measure 1½ in. up from the segment you drew in step 4 and draw a pair of horizontal parallel segments 1 in. apart, connecting the vertical segments you drew in step 2.	**-94:** • Measure ¾ in. up from the segment you drew in step 4 and draw a pair of horizontal parallel segments ½ in. apart, connecting the vertical segments you drew in step 2.

Follow-the-Directions Solve & Draw Math, Grades 6–8 • © 2009 by Merideth Anderson • Scholastic Teaching Resources

Step/Question	If your answer is . . .	
6 Make the buckle.	**57:** • Set your compass for a 3-in.-diameter circle. • On the left side of the parallel segments you drew in step 5, draw a circle. • Erase the line segments inside the circle.	**-163:** • On the left side of the parallel segments you drew in step 5, draw a 1¾-in. square. • Erase the line segments inside the square.
7 Make the buckle.	**1,003:** • Set your compass for a 1-in-diameter circle. • In the center of the circle you drew in step 6, draw a circle. • Erase all the segments within the circles.	**-3,607:** • In the center of the square you drew in step 6, draw a rectangle with a base of ¾ in. and a height of 1¼ in. • Erase the parallel segments you drew in step 5 inside the square and the rectangle (steps 6 and 7).
8 Make the brim.	**52:** • From the left endpoint of the top segment you drew in step 5, measure up ¼ in., and make a mark. • Use the segment you drew in step 2 as a base and this point as a vertex to make a 72° angle. Draw a 1⅜-in. oblique segment extending down and to the left.	**-156:** • From the left endpoint of the top segment you drew in step 5, measure up 1 in., and make a mark. • Use the segment you drew in step 2 as a base and this point as a vertex to make an 80° angle. Draw a 1¾-in. oblique segment extending down and to the left.
9 Make the brim.	**-840:** • Use the segment you drew in step 8 as a base and its left endpoint as a vertex to make a 142° angle. Draw a 2½-in. oblique segment extending down and to the left.	**840:** • Use the segment you drew in step 8 as a base and its left endpoint as a vertex to make a 130° angle. Draw a 1½-in. oblique segment extending down and to the left.
10 Make the brim.	**612:** • From the bottom of the segment you drew in step 9, draw a 2-in. vertical segment extending down.	**-612:** • From the bottom of the segment you drew in step 9, draw a 1¼-in. vertical segment extending down.

Step/Question	If your answer is . . .	
11 Make the brim.	**-45:** • Use the segment you drew in step 10 as a base and its bottom endpoint as a vertex to make a 150° angle. Draw a 2½-in. oblique line segment extending down and to the right.	**45:** • Use the segment you drew in step 10 as a base and its bottom endpoint as a vertex to make a 133° angle. Draw a 1⅞-in. oblique line segment extending down and to the right.
12 Make the brim.	**4,896:** • From the bottom endpoint of the segment you drew in step 11, draw a 6⅝-in. horizontal segment extending right.	**-4,896:** • From the bottom endpoint of the segment you drew in step 11, draw an 8½-in. horizontal segment extending right
13 Make the brim.	**7:** • Use the segment you drew in step 12 as a base and its right endpoint as a vertex to make a 30° angle. Draw a 2½-in. oblique segment extending up and to the right.	**-7:** • Use the segment you drew in step 12 as a base and its right endpoint as a vertex to make a 150° angle. Draw a 1⅞-in. oblique segment extending up and to the right.
14 Make the brim.	**53:** • Use the segment you drew in step 13 as a base and its top endpoint as a vertex to make a 45° angle. Draw a 2-in. oblique line segment extending up and to the right.	**-53:** • Use the segment you drew in step 13 as a base and its top endpoint as a vertex to make a 135° angle. Draw a 1¼-in. oblique line segment extending up and to the right.
15 Make the brim.	**2:** • Use the segment you drew in step 14 as a base and its top endpoint as a vertex to make a 140° angle. Draw a 2¼-in. oblique segment extending up and to the right.	**-2:** • Use the segment you drew in step 14 as a base and its top endpoint as a vertex to make a 160° angle. Draw a 2-in. oblique segment extending up and to the right.
16 Make the brim.	**25:** • From the top endpoint of the segment you drew in step 15, draw a ½-in. oblique segment connecting to the four-leaf clover you drew in step 3.	**-25:** • From the top endpoint of the segment you drew in step 15, draw a 2-in. oblique segment connecting to the four-leaf clover you drew in step 3.

Follow-the-Directions Solve & Draw Math, Grades 6–8 • © 2009 by Merideth Anderson • Scholastic Teaching Resources

Racing Through Percents

Materials

* ✱ Racing Through Percents: Solve It (page 72)
* ✱ Racing Through Percents: Hidden Picture Directions (pages 73–77)
* ✱ Ruler
* ✱ Protractor
* ✱ Compass
* ✱ Copy paper (8½ x 14 or larger)
* ✱ Pencil

Vocabulary

Diameter: a segment passing through the center of a circle with its endpoints on the circle

Horizontal: parallel to the horizon (left to right)

Oblique segment: a segment that is neither vertical nor horizontal

Parallel segments: segments that lie in the same plane but never intersect

Quadrilateral: a four-sided polygon

Scalene triangle: a triangle with no equal sides

Segment: a part of a line with two endpoints

Vertical: perpendicular to the horizon (up and down)

Getting Started

1. Hand out copies of Racing Through Percents: Solve It and have students answer the problems.

2. When students have completed the practice page, hand out Racing Through Percents: Hidden Picture Directions. Review the steps with students and complete one or two steps with them, reminding them to take their time and read through the steps carefully.

3. To begin the drawing, have students collect the materials listed at left and set their papers horizontally (landscape).

4. If students are unfamiliar with using a compass to draw circles and arcs, model the procedure on page 6 before they begin drawing their hidden picture. Steps 3, 13, and 14 require the use of a compass.

5. If students are unfamiliar with using a protractor to draw angles, model the procedure on page 6 before students begin drawing their hidden picture. Steps 5, 6, 9, 10, 11, and 12 require the use of a protractor.

6. It may help students to draw a full circle for step 13 and then erase the top part of the circle to create an arc.

⚡ Fast Finishers

Have students who finish early decorate their car by writing a number and drawing advertisements on the side of the car. Incorporate writing in this activity by having students add to the following story starter: "Last night, I had a dream that I became a famous race car driver . . . ."

Answers (page 72)

1. 51.8	**9.** $3.25
2. 204	**10.** $179.40
3. 26.23	**11.** $0.97
4. 168	**12.** 40.8
5. 18.8	**13.** 32.4
6. $1.00	**14.** 72
7. $1.30	**15.** 23.75
8. $76.38	**16.** 21

Solution to Racing Through Percents

Name _____ Date _____

Directions: Solve each problem and show your work.

1 37% of 140	**2** 80% of 255	**3** 43% of 61	**4** 70% of 240
5 8% of 235	**6** 20% of $5.00	**7** 13% of $9.99	**8** 67% of $114.00
9 25% of $12.98	**10** 30% of $598.00	**11** 65% of $1.49	**12** 120% of 34
13 27% of 120	**14** 60% of 120	**15** 25% of 95	**16** 7% of 300

Directions: Use your answers to Racing Through Percents: Solve It to choose an answer for each step below. One step at a time, follow the directions to reveal the hidden picture.

Step/Question	If your answer is . . .	
1 Make the bottom.	**5.18:** • In the center of the page, 3 in. from the bottom, draw a 10-in. horizontal segment.	**51.8:** • In the center of the page, 3 in. from the bottom, draw a 14½-in. horizontal segment
2 Make the wheels.	**20.4:** • On the segment you drew in step 1, make two marks: one 2 in. to the right of the left endpoint and the other 2 in. to the left of the right endpoint.	**204:** • On the segment you drew in step 1, make two marks: one 3½ in. to the right of the left endpoint and the other 4 in. to the left of the right endpoint.
3 Make the wheels.	**26.23:** • Set your compass for a 4-in.-diameter circle. • Place the sharp tip of the compass on each mark you made in step 2, and draw a circle. • Erase the segment inside the circle.	**2.623:** • Set your compass for a 3-in.-diameter circle. • Place the sharp tip of the compass on each mark you made in step 2, and draw a circle. • Erase the segment inside the circle.
4 Make the front-end.	**168:** • From the right endpoint of the segment you drew in step 1, draw a ½-in. vertical segment extending up.	**16.8:** • From the right endpoint of the segment you drew in step 1, draw a 1-in. vertical segment extending up.
5 Make the body.	**188:** • Use the segment you drew in step 4 as a base and its top endpoint as a vertex. Measure a 116° angle, drawing a 4-in. oblique line segment extending up and to the left.	**18.8:** • Use the segment you drew in step 4 as a base and its top endpoint as a vertex. Measure a 116° angle, drawing a 6⁷⁄₁₆-in. oblique line segment extending up and to the left.
6 Make the body.	**$1.00:** • Use the segment you drew in step 5 as a base and its top endpoint as a vertex. Measure a 170° angle, drawing a 2⅝-in. oblique line segment extending up and to the left.	**$0.10:** • Use the segment you drew in step 5 as a base and its top endpoint as a vertex. Measure a 170° angle, drawing a 3-in. oblique line segment extending up and to the left.

Step/Question		
⑦ Make the windshield. △ **7** or △ **7** 6 6	**$1.30:** • Toward the top of the segment you drew in step 6, draw a scalene right triangle with a base of 1⅛ in., a height of ½ in., and the third side 1¼ in. The long tip should point down.	**$0.13:** • Toward the top of the segment you drew in step 6, draw an equilateral triangle with 1-in. sides.
⑧ Make the body. 8 └──── 1	**$7.60:** • Place your pencil on the left endpoint of the segment you drew in step 1. • Draw a 1-in. vertical segment extending up.	**$76.38:** • Place your pencil on the left endpoint of the segment you drew in step 1. • Draw a 1⁹⁄₁₆-in. vertical segment extending up.
⑨ Make the body. 9 8	**$2.60** • Use the segment you drew in step 8 as a base and its top endpoint as a vertex. Measure a 127° angle, drawing a 1-in. oblique line segment extending up and to the right.	**$3.25:** • Use the segment you drew in step 8 as a base and its top endpoint as a vertex. Measure a 127° angle, drawing a 1⅝-in. oblique line segment extending up and to the right.
⑩ Make the body. 10 9	**$179.40:** • Use the segment you drew in step 9 as a base and its top endpoint as a vertex. Measure a 172° angle, drawing a 1-in. oblique line segment extending up and to the right.	**$17.94:** • Use the segment you drew in step 9 as a base and its top endpoint as a vertex. Measure a 172° angle, drawing a 2-in. oblique line segment extending up and to the right.
⑪ Make the body. 11 10	**$9.70:** • Use the segment you drew in step 10 as a base and its top endpoint as a vertex. Measure a 173° angle, drawing a 2-in. oblique line segment extending up and to the right.	**$0.97:** • Use the segment you drew in step 10 as a base and its top endpoint as a vertex. Measure a 173° angle, drawing a 1⅝-in. oblique line segment extending up and to the right.
⑫ Make the body. 12 11	**408:** • Use the segment you drew in step 11 as a base and its top endpoint as a vertex. Measure a 140° angle, drawing a 2½-in. oblique line segment extending up and to the right.	**40.8:** • Use the segment you drew in step 11 as a base and its top endpoint as a vertex. Measure a 165° angle, drawing a ⅞-in. oblique line segment extending up and to the right.

Follow-the-Directions Solve & Draw Math, Grades 6–8 • © 2009 by Merideth Anderson • Scholastic Teaching Resources

Step/Question	If your answer is . . .	
13 Finish the body.	**32.4:** • Set your compass for a 2-in.-diameter circle. • Placing the pencil tip on the right endpoint of the segment you drew in step 12, draw a downward arc that connects to the left endpoint of the segment you drew in step 6.	**32:** • Set your compass for a 3-in.-diameter circle. • Placing the pencil tip on the right endpoint of the segment you drew in step 12, draw a downward arc that connects to the left endpoint of the segment you drew in step 6.
14 Make the driver.	**72:** • Set your compass for a 1-in.-diameter circle. • Draw a circle inside the arc you drew in step 13. (The bottom of the circle should not intersect the bottom of the arc.)	**48:** • Set your compass for a 2-in.-diameter circle. • Draw a circle inside the arc you drew in step 13. (The bottom of the circle should not intersect the bottom of the arc.)
15 Make the driver.	**71.25:** • Draw a pair of perpendicular segments connecting the bottom of the circle you drew in step 14 to the bottom of the arc you drew in step 13.	**23.75:** • Draw a pair of vertical parallel segments connecting the bottom of the circle you drew in step 14 to the bottom of the arc you drew in step 13.
16 Make the facemask.	**21:** • Inside the circle you drew in step 14, draw an acute angle with endpoints that fall on the right side of the circle.	**210:** • Inside the circle you drew in step 14, draw a rectangle with one side whose corners fall on the right side of the circle. • Erase the fourth side.

Fraction Factions

Materials

* Fraction Factions: Solve It (page 77)
* Fraction Factions: Hidden Picture Directions (pages 78–81)
* Ruler
* Protractor
* Compass
* Copy paper (8 ½ x 14 or larger)
* Pencil

Vocabulary

Horizontal: parallel to the horizon (left to right)

Isosceles triangles: a triangle with exactly two equal sides

Oblique segment: a segment that is neither vertical nor horizontal

Parallel segments: segments that lie in the same plane but do not intersect

Perpendicular segments: segments that intersect to form right angles

Segment: a part of a line with two endpoints

Semicircle: a half of a circle

Simplified: reduced

Vertical: perpendicular to the horizon (up and down)

Getting Started

1. Hand out copies of Fraction Factions: Solve It and have students answer the problems.

2. When students have completed the practice page, hand out Fraction Factions: Hidden Picture Directions. Review the steps with students and complete one or two steps with them, reminding them to take their time and read through the steps carefully.

3. To begin the drawing, have students collect the materials listed at left, set their papers horizontally (landscape), and fold their paper in half horizontally. This activity has a picture on each half of the page. Steps 1–9 give instruction to draw the elephant on the left-hand side of the page, and steps 10–16 are for the donkey on the right-hand side of the page.

4. If students are unfamiliar with using a compass to draw circles and arcs, model the procedure on page 6 before they begin drawing their hidden picture. Step 1 requires the use of a compass.

5. If students are unfamiliar with using a protractor to draw angles, model the procedure on page 6 before students begin drawing their hidden picture. Steps 6, 7, 11, and 13 require the use of a protractor.

⚡ Fast Finishers

Have students who finish early use their knowledge of geometry and patriotic colors to finish their picture by including the following in their design: a concave decagon seen on the United States flag (at least one on each animal), a ½-in. circle representing the animal's eye (one on each animal), and a background decorated in a creative way to show patriotism.

Solution to Fraction Factions

Answers (page 77)

1. $\frac{9}{10}$ or 0.9	**9.** $\frac{12}{23}$ or 0.52
2. 9	**10.** $\frac{6}{13}$ or 0.46
3. $94\frac{23}{24}$ or 94.96	**11.** 42
4. $30\frac{15}{16}$ or 30.94	**12.** $1\frac{2}{3}$ or 1.67
5. 18	**13.** 30
6. 54	**14.** $\frac{2}{3}$ or 0.67
7. $1\frac{1}{2}$ or 1.5	**15.** 1,053
8. $\frac{2}{7}$ or 0.29	**16.** $18\frac{2}{3}$ or 18.67

Name _____ Date _____

Directions: Solve each problem and show your work.

1 $\frac{3}{5} \times 1\frac{1}{2}$	**2** $2\frac{2}{3} \times 3\frac{3}{8}$	**3** $8\frac{5}{6} \times 10\frac{3}{4}$	**4** $3\frac{1}{8} \times 9\frac{9}{10}$
5 $10 \times 1\frac{4}{5}$	**6** $42 \div \frac{7}{9}$	**7** $4\frac{7}{8} \div 3\frac{1}{4}$	**8** $\frac{6}{7} \div 3$
9 $2\frac{2}{3} \div 5\frac{1}{9}$	**10** $1\frac{1}{5} \div 2\frac{3}{5}$	**11** $\frac{1}{8} d = 5\frac{1}{4}$	**12** $3w = 5$
13 $y \div 12 = 2\frac{1}{2}$	**14** $b \div 1\frac{1}{3} = \frac{1}{2}$	**15** $117 = \frac{1}{9u}$	**16** $s \div 8 = 2\frac{1}{3}$

Directions: Use your answers to Fraction Factions: Solve It to choose an answer for each step below. One step at a time, follow the directions to reveal the hidden picture.

* **Before you start, fold your paper in half as shown here. You will be drawing 2 different pictures. Each picture will take up half the page.**

Step/Question	If your answer is . . .	
1 Draw the top of the elephant. 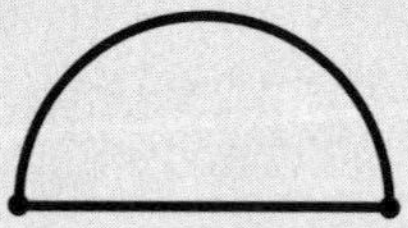	**$1\frac{3}{10}$:** • On the left half of the page, measure down 4½ in. from the top. • Draw a 4-in. horizontal line segment (centered horizontally). • Draw a 4-in.-diameter semicircle above the segment connecting the two endpoints.	**$\frac{9}{10}$:** • On the left half of the page, measure down 4½ in. from the top. • Draw a 6-in. horizontal line segment (centered horizontally). • Draw a 6-in.-diameter semicircle above the segment connecting the two endpoints.
2 Make the body. 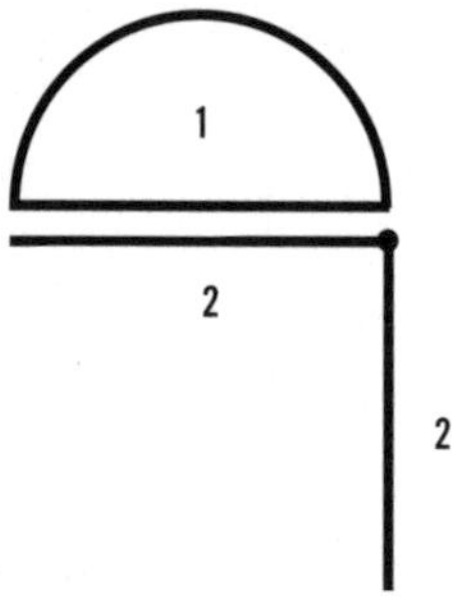	**9:** • Positioned ¼ in. below and parallel to the segment you drew in step 1, draw a 6-in. segment. • From the right endpoint of this segment, draw a 5-in. vertical segment extending down.	**$6\frac{1}{4}$:** • Positioned ¼ in. below and parallel to the segment you drew in step 1, draw a 7-in. segment. • From the right endpoint of this segment, draw a 3-in. vertical segment extending down.
3 Make the hind leg. 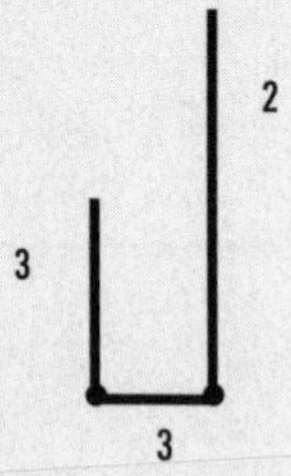	**$\frac{106}{129}$:** • From the bottom endpoint of the vertical segment you drew in step 2, draw a 2-in. horizontal segment extending left. • From the left endpoint of this segment, draw a 1-in. vertical segment extending up.	**$94\frac{23}{24}$:** • From the bottom endpoint of the vertical segment you drew in step 2, draw a 1-in. horizontal segment extending left. • From the left endpoint of this segment, draw a 2-in. vertical segment extending up.
4 Make the body. 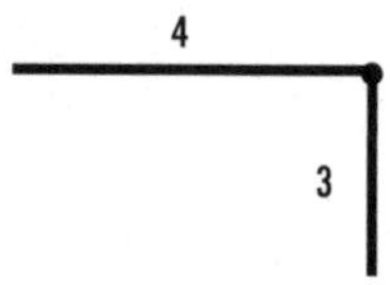	**$27\frac{9}{80}$:** • From the top endpoint of the vertical segment you drew in step 3, draw a 1-in. horizontal segment extending left.	**$30\frac{15}{16}$:** • From the top endpoint of the vertical segment you drew in step 3, draw a 3-in. horizontal segment extending left.

Follow-the-Directions Solve & Draw Math, Grades 6–8 • © 2009 by Merideth Anderson • Scholastic Teaching Resources

Step/Question	If your answer is . . .	
5 Make the front leg.	**18:** • From the left endpoint of the segment you drew in step 4, draw a 2-in. vertical segment extending down. • From the bottom endpoint of this segment, draw a 1-in. horizontal segment extending left. • From the left endpoint of the second segment, draw a 2-in. vertical segment extending up.	**⁹⁄₅₀:** • From the left endpoint of the segment you drew in step 4, draw a 3-in. vertical segment extending down. • From the bottom endpoint of this segment, draw a 2-in. horizontal segment extending left. • From the left endpoint of the second segment, draw a 3-in. vertical segment extending up.
6 Make the trunk.	**32⅔:** • Use the final segment you drew in step 5 as a base and the top endpoint as a vertex to make a 35° angle. Draw a 1-in. oblique segment extending down and left.	**54:** • Use the final segment you drew in step 5 as a base and the top endpoint as a vertex to make a 50° angle. Draw a 2¾-in. oblique segment extending down and left.
7 Make the trunk.	**1½:** • Use the segment you drew in step 6 as a base and the bottom endpoint as a vertex to make a 53° angle. Draw a 3-in. oblique segment extending up and left.	**1²³⁄₃₂:** • Use the segment you drew in step 6 as a base and the bottom endpoint as a vertex to make a 40° angle. Draw a 2-in. oblique segment extending up and left.
8 Make the trunk.	**²⁄₇:** • From the top endpoint of the segment you drew in step 7, draw a ¾-in horizontal segment extending right.	**⁶⁄₂₁:** • From the top endpoint of the segment you drew in step 7, draw a 1½-in horizontal segment extending right.
9 Finish the elephant.	**1¹¹⁄₁₂:** • From the right endpoint of the segment you drew in step 8, draw a 1-in. vertical segment extending down. • Connect the bottom endpoint with the left endpoint of the segment you drew in step 2 (an approximately 5-in oblique segment).	**¹²⁄₂₃:** • From the right endpoint of the segment you drew in step 8, draw a 1¾-in. vertical segment extending down. • Connect the bottom endpoint with the left endpoint of the segment you drew in step 2 (an approximately 3¾-in. oblique segment).

✱ **Now you will begin a second drawing on the right side of the paper.**

Step/Question	If your answer is . . .	
10 Make the donkey's body. [ ] **or** [ ]	**3 ³⁄₂₅:** • Measure down 3½ in. from the top of the page and ¾ in. to the right of the center fold of the page. • This point will be the top left corner of a square you draw with 5-in. sides.	**⁶⁄₁₃:** • Measure down 3½ in. from the top of the page and ¾ in. to the right of the center fold of the page. • This point will be the top left corner of a rectangle you draw with a base of 5 in. and height of 2 in.
11 Make the neck.	**5 ¹⁄₃₂:** • Use the top of the figure you drew in step 10 as the base and the right endpoint as a vertex to make a 125° angle. Draw a 1-in. oblique segment extending up and right. • Use the bottom of the figure you drew in step 10 as the base and the right endpoint as a vertex to make a 110° angle. Draw a 3-in. segment extending up and right. • Connect the endpoints of these segments.	**42:** • Use the top of the figure you drew in step 10 as the base and the right endpoint as a vertex to make a 145° angle. Draw a 2¾-in. oblique segment extending up and right. • Use the bottom of the figure you drew in step 10 as the base and the right endpoint as a vertex to make a 130° angle. Draw a 3⅝-in. segment extending up and right. • Connect the endpoints of these segments.
12 Make the ears.	**15:** • Use the last segment you drew in step 11 as the base of an isosceles triangle, with the equal sides measuring ½ in. • Make a second ear with the same dimensions at the end of the top line segment you drew in step 11.	**1⅔:** • Use the last segment you drew in step 11 as the base of an isosceles triangle, with the equal sides measuring 1¼ in. • Make a second ear with the same dimensions at the end of the top line segment you drew in step 11.

Follow-the-Directions Solve & Draw Math, Grades 6–8 • © 2009 by Merideth Anderson • Scholastic Teaching Resources